the Reflective Educator's Guide to Classroom Research

the **Reflective Educator's Guide to Classroom Research**

*Learning to Teach and Teaching to Learn
Through Practitioner Inquiry*

NANCY FICHTMAN DANA, 1964-   DIANE YENDOL-SILVA

Foreword by Ann Lieberman

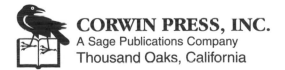

CORWIN PRESS, INC.
A Sage Publications Company
Thousand Oaks, California

For information:

Corwin Press, Inc.
A Sage Publications Company
2455 Teller Road
Thousand Oaks, California 91320
www.corwinpress.com

Sage Publications Ltd.
6 Bonhill Street
London EC2A 4PU
United Kingdom

Sage Publications India Pvt. Ltd.
B-42, Panchsheel Enclave
Post Box 4109
New Delhi 110 017 India

Printed in the United States of America

Library of Congress Cataloging-in-Publication Data

Dana, Nancy Fichtman, 1964-
The reflective educator's guide to classroom research: Learning to teach and teaching to learn through practitioner inquiry / Nancy Fichtman Dana, Diane Yendol-Silva.
         p. cm.
Includes bibliographical references and index.
ISBN 0-7619-4645-4 -- ISBN 0-7619-4646-2 (pbk.)
1. Action research in education. 2. Teachers-In-service training.
      I. Yendol-Silva, Diane. II. Title.
LB1028.24.D36 2003
370′.7′2--dc21
2002156157

05   06   10   9   8   7   6   5   4

Acquisitions Editor:	Faye Zucker
Editorial Assistants:	Julia Parnell/Stacy Wagner
Production Editor:	Melanie Birdsall
Copy Editor:	Dana Polachowski
Typesetter:	C&M Digitals (P) Ltd.
Indexer:	Sheila Bodell
Proofreader:	Kristin Bergstad
Cover Designer:	Michael Dubowe

Contents

Foreword

The Reflective Educator's Guide to Classroom Research is more than a book about how to do teacher research or action research in your own classroom. Certainly it is that, but it is much more than that. Building on the awareness that teachers have an enormous amount of knowledge that they have accumulated through their years of teaching, the authors show how this knowledge can be mined by teachers studying their own practice, making visible the complexities of teaching. It is work that is enriched by sharing with other teachers who can learn from it, expand it, critique it, and build upon it. By learning about their practice in this way, teachers not only build their capacity to better understand their own teaching, but also help to build a collaborative culture in their school.

This kind of practitioner inquiry requires teachers to have access to some kind of a group, either inside or outside their school, so that an "inquiry stance" toward teaching becomes a way of life. There is increasing evidence that some teachers who study their practice, go public with their teaching, and share what they are learning with colleagues not only develop greater confidence and understanding about their own teaching and student learning, but also begin to think differently about what it means to be a "life long learner" (Lieberman & Wood, 2002).

A special quality of the writing in this book makes us feel that Nancy Dana and Diane Yendol-Silva are two friends by our side, helping us to develop a process for thinking about teaching and learning in our own classrooms. Numerous authors have attempted to write "how to" books about teacher research, but this one recognizes that doing research is a process, and that the role of the authors is to engage the reader in moving through that process: how you get from a *focus* on a particular student who keeps you awake at night, or something in the curriculum or the interaction of students, to the development of a way of studying the problem that eventually illuminates its complexities and often leads to ways of thinking that suggest actions, strategies, and solutions. It is apparent that the authors have facilitated classroom research involving many teachers, as the processes we read about are rooted in the reality of teachers' struggles to know more about their teaching and to get better at understanding their own as well as their students' motivations to learn.

The Reflective Educator's Guide to Classroom Research helps us learn that collaborating with peers helps not only one's own research quest, but that it can be the source of better group understanding as well. Do we want to do a *shared* inquiry? a *parallel* inquiry where we do our own research, as others do theirs by looking at the same topic? or an *intersecting* inquiry where people have different questions on the same topic? How can we learn to do research as a part of teaching work and not an add-on? What strategies can we develop to collect data? And once data are collected, the common question "What do I do with all this information?" The authors are right there: teaching, facilitating, supporting, and moving us through a variety of ways to look at data, always grounded in teacher examples and always explicated by conceptual understandings of how to think about each of these steps.

Readers of this book experience not only what it is like to do classroom research, but perhaps as important, gain an understanding of how teachers can become scholars of their own practice. These "scholars" become colleagues capable of developing their own means of holding themselves accountable within the context of a professional learning community; a community of teachers (as well as their students) excited about learning and stimulated by their continuous inquiries into their own practice.

Ann Lieberman
Senior Scholar, Carnegie Foundation
for the Advancement of Teaching
Visiting Professor, Stanford University

REFERENCE

Lieberman, Ann, & Wood, Diane R. (2002). The National Writing Project. *Educational Leadership* 59 (6), pp. 40-43.

Preface

What is teacher inquiry and why is it important?

What might teacher inquiry look like?

What is the relationship between teacher inquiry and teacher professional growth?

How do schools and universities work together to provide a context for teacher inquiry?

If you are a member of a public school or university teacher education community—intern, student teacher, mentor teacher, administrator, or teacher educator—you join hundreds of other educators across the nation who are currently contemplating these and other serious questions about teacher inquiry as a tool for professional growth. These are timely questions since we are living in an era where prescriptive policies and curriculum created through the political process in the name of public accountability are complicating school-level responsiveness to student needs as well as opportunities for teacher knowledge construction (Darling-Hammond, 1994). Inquiry by teachers in their own classrooms provides a viable tool for "challenging these current assumptions about how teachers learn and about what constitutes a knowledge base for teaching" (Cochran-Smith & Lytle, 1993, p. 2).

As critical as the teacher inquiry role is to reforming teaching and teacher education, we know from studies across the nation that the teacher-inquirer role has been slow to develop (see, e.g., Frankes, Valli, & Cooper, 1998). We believe that by sharing what we have learned from practicing and prospective teachers' conceptions of teacher inquiry, examples of their inquiry work, and evidence of their reform-minded teaching that the process of inquiry can spread to new classrooms across the country. As a result, this book has been created to help prospective and practicing teaching professionals understand the process of inquiry, develop as teacher-inquirers, and engage in reform-minded teaching.

This book emerges from our understanding of the literature in the area of professional development, action research, teacher research, qualitative research, and the process of change as well as our collective experience working with practicing and prospective teachers engaged in inquiry since the mid-1980s. What we have learned from these teachers about how and why they inquire provides insights into the power teacher inquiry holds to transform classrooms and schools to places where teachers' voices contribute to the knowledge that is generated about teaching and learning.

ABOUT THIS BOOK

Using a journey metaphor, in this text we take you through the process of inquiry step by step. You begin your journey with a brief introduction to teacher inquiry in Chapter 1 and then move to Chapter 2 to define your first inquiry. This chapter, appropriately entitled "The Start of Your Journey: Finding a Wondering," gets you started on an inquiry by engaging you in a series of exercises designed to help you cut through all of the intricacies and complexities of teaching to "focus in" on one area that you are passionate about studying. We define eight passions as places where you may locate your wondering. These passions include inquiring into an individual child, a desire to improve curriculum, a desire to enhance content knowledge, a desire to improve or experiment with teaching strategies and teaching techniques, a desire to explore the relationship between your beliefs and your classroom practice, an investigation of the intersection between your personal and professional identities, issues of social justice, and understanding the learning context. As we explore each passion, we utilize examples from teacher-inquirers we have worked with to illustrate the ways their wonderings emerged from the intersection of their real-world classroom experiences and one of the particular passions defined in Chapter 2.

In Chapter 3, we explore the importance of collaboration with other educators and define four possible structures for inquiry collaboration that might support your inquiry work. At the close of this chapter, you will be ready to begin data collection, a process that is explored in Chapter 4. In this chapter, we discuss seven common strategies for data collection utilized by teacher-inquirers (fieldnotes, document analysis, interviews, focus groups, reflective journals, surveys, and literature).

Throughout our discussion, we point to the ways each of these strategies connects to what you already do in your life and work as a teacher. We do this because we want you to see how teacher inquiry is *a part of,* not *apart from,* the work you do as a teacher.

In Chapter 5, we explore what we have found to be one of the most difficult steps for teacher-inquirers—data analysis. If you enjoy jigsaw puzzles you will particularly enjoy your journey through this chapter, as we fully develop this metaphor to describe the data analysis process step by step. In addition, we use the work of one teacher-inquirer to illustrate what data analysis might actually look like in practice.

In Chapter 6, we look closely at the "writing it up process" as a way to extend the learning that has occurred during data analysis. One teacher-inquirer's work is shared in its entirety to illustrate four basic components of any teacher's inquiry write-up.

Finally, in Chapter 7, we bring closure to your first inquiry journey by discussing the importance of sharing your inquiry with others and helping you identify outlets for your work.

Across the nation, prospective and practicing teachers vary greatly in their experience with teacher inquiry. Perhaps you are brand new to teacher inquiry. Perhaps you have been engaged in inquiry for years and wish to further the development of teacher inquiry in your school. Perhaps you wish to make teacher inquiry a more visible or meaningful part of your teacher education program. Perhaps you seek to mentor other professionals in their first inquiries. Wherever you may be in your inquiry journey, we hope this text provides the impetus for you to take the next steps along the pathway of simultaneous renewal and reform. Happy Inquiring!

ACKNOWLEDGMENTS

We have had the honor and privilege to work with many tremendous teachers throughout our careers, and it is through these teachers' work that we have witnessed the process of inquiry and the power of inquiry as a tool for professional learning. Throughout our careers, we have also always been passionate about raising the voices of teachers in educational reform, teaching, and teacher education. In an effort to raise teacher voices, we weave within this text many rich examples of these teachers' inquiries as we describe the process step by step. Hence, this book would not have been possible without the inquiries that only prospective and practicing teachers can provide. We are grateful to all of the practicing teachers in the State College Area School District-Pennsylvania State University

Elementary Professional Development School Program, Alachua Elementary School, PK Yonge Developmental School, and the Northeast Zone of the Broward County School District, as well as the Penn State–State College Area School District Elementary PDS interns, and University of Florida Democracy Diversity, and Literacy (DDL) Community preinterns. Their time, dedication, and contribution to teacher inquiry and the education profession are immeasurable. We continue to admire their devotion and are grateful for their dedication to the profession of teaching and their support in writing this book.

Much of this book was drafted at a Woman's Research Retreat. We wish to thank the women who invited us to be a part of this wonderful week and provided support, the right word when needed, great conceptual discussion, and most of all friendship as this book was in its early stages— Carla Zembal-Saul, Pat and Claire Friedrichsen, Leigh Ann Haefner, Lucy Avraamidou, and Dawn McGonigal (and Avery and Boone).

Finally, we wish to thank Penn State's Hermanowicz Professor of Teacher Education and a wonderful colleague (Nancy's husband) and friend—Tom Dana. He continues to lay the foundation for our professional development school work and the spread of teacher inquiry that we began at Penn State with his unselfish support and encouragement in the early stages of our work. The many conversations we had as this book was taking shape were invaluable to its completion. He served as our computer consultant, editor, idea-bouncer, and friend. We are grateful for and admire his dedication to rethinking teacher education and building an inquiry stance toward teaching, as well as his awesome administrative talent that make these things happen.

Corwin Press gratefully acknowledges the contributions of the following reviewers:

Ismat Abdal-Haqq
Manager
Education Technology Publications
National School Boards Association
Alexandria, VA

Mary Ann Coe
Associate Professor
West College of Education
Midwestern State University
Wichita Falls, TX

Robert Bulik
Associate Professor of Family Medicine
Department of Family Medicine
Office of Educational Development
University of Texas Medical Branch
Galveston, TX

Sid Trubowitz
Professor
School of Education
Queens College
City University of New York
New York, NY

Mimi Gilman
Educational Technology Consultant
Adjunct Professor
Lesley University
Saratoga, WY

Rachel Hungerford
Assistant Professor and Department Chair
Department of Education
Lycoming College
Williamsport, PA

About the Authors

Nancy Fichtman Dana is currently a Professor of Education at the University of Florida, where she facilitates school-university partnership work across the College of Education. Before joining the University of Florida, she was an Associate Professor of Education at Pennsylvania State University, where she developed and codirected the State College Area School District–Pennsylvania State University Elementary Professional Development School Program. She holds a Ph.D. in Elementary Education from Florida State University. She began her career in education as an elementary school teacher in Hannibal Central Schools, New York, and has worked closely with elementary school teachers on teacher inquiry and school-university collaborations in Florida and Pennsylvania since 1990. She has authored numerous articles in professional journals, focusing on teacher inquiry, teacher leadership, school–university collaboration, and professional development schools. Nancy Dana may be reached via the Internet at ndana@coe.ufl.edu.

Diane Yendol-Silva is currently an Assistant Professor of Education at the University of Florida and partner in the Diversity, Democracy, and Literacy Communities (DDL). She holds a Ph.D. in Curriculum and Instruction from The Pennsylvania State University. Diane spent 13 years as an elementary school teacher. While completing her doctorate at Penn State, Diane had the opportunity to work in the professional development schools initiated by Nancy Fichtman Dana and today spreads the work Nancy taught her as she works with teachers in Florida. Diane is currently developing school-university partnerships and communities of inquiry with partnering schools in Florida. She has authored articles in professional journals focusing on creating communities of inquiry, teacher leadership, mentoring, and school-university collaboration. Diane Yendol-Silva may be reached via the Internet at dsilva@coe.ufl.edu.

For our children,
who keep our passion for reforming teaching
and teacher education alive—Greg, Kirsten, Caran, and Billy

Teacher Inquiry Defined   1

Teaching involves a search for meaning in the world. Teaching is a life project, a calling, a vocation that is an organizing center of all other activities. Teaching is past and future as well as present, it is background as well as foreground, it is depth as well as surface. Teaching is pain and humor, joy and anger, dreariness and epiphany. Teaching is world building, it is architecture and design, it is purpose and moral enterprise. Teaching is a way of being in the world that breaks through the boundaries of the traditional job and in the process redefines all life and teaching itself.

— William Ayers

Whether you are a beginning teacher, veteran teacher, administrator, or teacher educator, when you think of teaching, learning to teach, and continuing one's growth as a teacher, you cannot help but be struck by the enormous complexities, paradoxes, and tensions that exist in the simple act of teaching itself, captured so eloquently in the quote from William Ayers. With all of these complexities, paradoxes, and tensions, a teacher's work shapes the daily life of his or her classroom. In addition to responding to the needs of the children within the classroom, a teacher is expected to implement the endless changes advocated by those outside the four walls of the classroom—administrators, politicians, and researchers. While teachers have gained insights into their educational practice from these three groups, the voices of teachers have typically been absent from the larger discussions about educational change and reform. Historically teachers have not had access to tools that could have brought their knowledge to the table and raised their voices to a high-enough level in these larger conversations. Teacher inquiry is a vehicle that can be used by teachers to untangle some of the complexity that occurs in the profession, raise teachers' voices in discussions of educational reform, and ultimately transform assumptions about the teaching profession itself. Transforming the profession is really the capstone to the teacher inquiry story. Let's begin our journey into the what, why, and how of teacher inquiry with an overview of the evolution of the teacher inquiry movement and a simple definition of this very complex, rewarding, transformative, provocative, and productive process.

WHAT IS TEACHER INQUIRY?

Understanding the history of teacher inquiry can help you recognize how, as a current or future educator, you find yourself today investigating a new paradigm of learning that can lead to educational renewal and reform. This history lesson begins by looking closely at three educational research traditions: process-product research, qualitative or interpretive research, and teacher inquiry (see Table 1.1).

Two paradigms have dominated educational research on schooling, teaching, and learning over the past two decades. In the first paradigm, the underlying conception of "process-product research" (Shulman, 1986) portrays teaching as a primarily linear activity and depicts teachers as technicians. The teacher's role is to implement the research findings of "outside" experts, almost exclusively university researchers, who are considered alien to the everyday happenings in classrooms. In this transmissive mode teachers are not expected to be problem-posers or problem-solvers. Rather, teachers negotiate dilemmas framed by outside experts and are asked to implement with fidelity a curriculum designed by those outside of the classroom. Based on this paradigm, many teachers have learned that it is sometimes best not to problematize their lived classroom experiences or first-hand observations because to do so may mean an admittance of failure to implement curriculum as directed. In fact, the transmissive culture of many schools has demonstrated that teachers can suffer punitive repercussions from highlighting areas that teachers themselves identify as problematic. The consequences of pointing out problems have often resulted in traditional top-down "retraining" or remediation. In the transmissive view, our educational community does not encourage solution-seeking behavior on the part of classroom teachers.

In the second paradigm, educational research drawn from qualitative or interpretative studies, teaching is portrayed as a highly complex, context-specific, interactive activity. In addition, this qualitative or interpretive

Table 1.1   Competing Paradigms: The Multiple Voices of Research

| | | *Research Paradigms* | |
	Process-Product	*Qualitative or Interpretive*	*Teacher Inquiry*
Teacher	Teacher as technician	Teacher as story character	Teacher as story teller
Researcher	Outsider	Outsider	Insider
Process	Linear	Discursive	Cyclical
Source of research question	Researcher	Researcher	Teacher
Type of research question	Focused on control, prediction, or impact	Focused on explaining a process or phenomenon	Focused on providing insight into a teacher's classroom practice in an effort to make change
Example of research question	Which management strategy is most successful?	How do children experience bullying in the classroom?	How can I accommodate ESL students at the kindergarten writing table?

paradigm captures differences across classrooms, schools, and communities that are critically important. Chris Clark (1995) identifies the complexity inherent in a teacher's job and the importance of understanding and acknowledging contextual differences as follows: "Description becomes prescription, often with less and less regard for the contextual matters that make the description meaningful in the first place" (p. 20).

Although qualitative or interpretive work attends to issues of context, most of these studies emerging from this research paradigm are conducted by university researchers and are intended for academic audiences. Such school-university research provides valuable insights into the connections between theory and practice but, like the process-product research, the qualitative or interpretive approach limits teachers' roles in the research process. In fact, the knowledge about teaching and learning generated through university study of theory and practice is still defined and generated by "outsiders" to the school and classroom. While both the process-product and qualitative research paradigms have generated valuable insights into the teaching and learning process, they have not included the voices of the people closest to the children—classroom teachers.

Hence, a third research tradition emerges highlighting the role classroom teachers play as knowledge-generators. This tradition is often referred to as "teacher research," "teacher inquiry," or "action research." In general, the teacher inquiry movement focuses on the concerns of teachers (not outside researchers) and engages teachers in the design, data collection, and interpretation of data around their question. Termed "action research" by Carr and Kemmis (1986), this approach to educational research has many benefits: (1) theories and knowledge are generated from research grounded in the realities of educational practice; (2) teachers become collaborators in educational research by investigating their own problems; and (3) teachers play a part in the research process, which makes them more likely to facilitate change based on the knowledge they create.

Elliot (1988) describes action research as a continual set of spirals consisting of reflection and action. Each spiral involves (1) clarifying and diagnosing a practical situation that needs to be improved or a practical problem that needs to be resolved; (2) formulating action strategies to improve the situation or resolve the problem; (3) implementing the action strategies and evaluating their effectiveness; and (4) clarifying the situation, resulting in new definitions of problems or areas for improvement, and so on, to the next spiral of reflection and action.

Now that we have explored three educational research traditions, acknowledged the limitations of the first two traditions, and introduced teacher inquiry, our brief history lesson might suggest that teacher inquiry is just another educational fad. However, although the terms *teacher research, action research,* and *teacher inquiry* are comparatively new, the underlying conceptions of teaching as inquiry and the role of teachers as inquirers are not. Early in the 20th century, John Dewey (1933) called for teachers to engage in "reflective action" that would transition them into inquiry-oriented classroom practitioners. Similarly, noted teacher educator Ken Zeichner (1996) traces and summarizes more than 30 years of research, calling for cultivating an informed practice as illustrated in such descriptors as "teachers as action researchers," "teacher scholars," "teacher innovators," and "teachers as participant observers" (p. 3). Similarly, distinguished scholar Donald Schon (1983, 1987) also depicts teacher professional practice as a cognitive process of posing and exploring problems or dilemmas identified by the teachers themselves. In doing so, teachers ask questions that other researchers may not perceive or deem relevant. In addition, teachers often discern patterns that "outsiders" may not be able to see.

Given today's political context, where much of the decision making and discussion regarding teachers occur outside the walls of the classroom (Darling-Hammond, 1994), the time seems ripe to create a movement where teachers are armed with the tools of inquiry and committed to educational change. If that is our goal, we now need to understand how teacher inquiry can serve as a tool for professional growth and educational reform. We believe that the simplest and most eloquently stated definitions of teacher research come from the work of two teacher-inquirers we have collaborated with; here are excerpts from their own journals:

> Teacher research enables me to investigate one of my wonderings in a deliberate fashion. I used the tools of a researcher to investigate my own environment. Teacher research provides the impetus for teachers to find various solutions to their own questions. By definition then, it is relevant inquiry. (Borst, 1999)

> Teacher research is a method of gaining insight from hindsight. It is a way of formalizing the questioning and reflecting we, as teachers, engage in every day in an attempt to improve student learning. (Brown, 1999)

WHAT IS THE RELATIONSHIP BETWEEN TEACHER INQUIRY AND TEACHER PROFESSIONAL GROWTH?

Simply stated, teacher inquiry is defined as systematic, intentional study of one's own professional practice (see, e.g., Cochran-Smith & Lytle, 1993; Dana, Gimbert, & Silva, 1999; Hubbard & Power, 1993). Inquiring professionals seek out change by reflecting on their practice. They do this by posing questions or "wonderings," collecting data to gain insights into their wonderings, analyzing the data along with reading relevant literature, making changes in practice based on new understandings developed during inquiry, and sharing findings with others. Hence, whether you are a prospective teacher at the dawn of your teaching career or a veteran teacher with years of experience facing new educational challenges every day, teacher inquiry becomes a powerful vehicle for learning and reform.

As a teacher-inquirer in charge of your own learning, you become a part of a larger struggle in education—the struggle to better understand, inform, shape, reshape, and reform standard school practice (Cochran-Smith, 1991). Teacher inquiry differs from traditional professional development for teachers, which has typically focused on the knowledge of an outside "expert" being shared with a group of teachers. This traditional model of professional growth, usually delivered as a part of traditional staff development, may appear an efficient method of disseminating information but often does not result in real and meaningful change in the classroom.

Those dissatisfied with the traditional model of professional development suggest a need for new approaches that enhance professional growth and lead to real change. For example, over 25 years ago, Goldhammer (1969) emphasized the need for supervision to become an opportunity to help teachers understand what they are doing, and why, by changing schools from places where teachers just act out "age-old rituals" to places where teachers participate fully in the process of supervision and their own professional growth. More recently, Nolan and Huber (1989) described teacher reflection, a key component of inquiry, as the "driving force" behind successful professional development programs. Nolan and Huber describe successful professional development programs as "making a difference in the lives and instruction of teachers who participate in them, as well as the lives of the students they teach" (p. 143).

Consonant with the movement to change traditional professional development practices is the teacher inquiry movement. This movement toward a new model of professional growth based on inquiry into one's own practice can be powerfully developed, by school districts and building administrators, as a form of professional development. By participating in teacher inquiry, the teacher develops a sense of ownership in the knowledge constructed, and this sense of ownership heavily contributes to the possibilities for real change to take place in the classroom.

The ultimate goal is to create an inquiry stance toward teaching. This stance becomes a professional positioning, owned by the teacher, where questioning one's own practice becomes part of the teacher's work and eventually a part of the teaching culture. By cultivating this inquiry stance toward teaching, teachers play a critical role in enhancing their own professional growth and ultimately the experience of schooling for children. Thus, an inquiry stance is synonymous with professional growth and provides a nontraditional approach to staff development that can lead to meaningful change for children.

HOW IS TEACHER INQUIRY DIFFERENT FROM WHAT I ALREADY DO AS A REFLECTIVE TEACHER?

All teachers reflect. They reflect on what happened during previously taught lessons as they plan lessons for the future. They reflect on their students' performance as they assess their work. They reflect on the content and the best pedagogy available to teach that content to their learners. They reflect about interactions they observed students having, as well as their own interactions with students and the ways these interactions contribute to learning. Teachers reflect all day, every day, while *in* the act of teaching and long after the school day is over *on* the act of teaching.

Reflection is important and critical to good teaching (Schon, 1987; Zeichner & Liston, 1996). In addition, reflection is a key component of teacher inquiry. Yet teacher inquiry is different from daily reflection in and on practice in two important ways. First, teacher inquiry is less happenstance. The very definition of teacher inquiry includes the word *intentional*. We do not mean to suggest that reflection is never intentional, but in the busy, complex life of teaching, reflection is something that occurs most often in an unplanned way, for example, on the way to the teacher's room for lunch, during a chat with a colleague during a special, when the students are engaged in an independent activity, on the drive home, in the shower, or during dinner—wherever and whenever a moment arises. Unfortunately, few teachers have a planned "reflection" time. Teacher inquiry invites intentional, planned reflection, heightening your focus on problem posing. Second, teacher inquiry is more visible. The daily reflection teachers engage in is not observable by others unless it is given some form (perhaps through talk or journaling). As teachers engage in the process of inquiry, their thinking and reflection are made public for discussion, sharing, debate, and purposeful educative conversation. As inquiry raises the visibility of teachers' thinking, the profession garners a new respect for the complexity teaching entails.

WHAT ARE SOME CONTEXTS THAT ARE RIPE FOR TEACHER INQUIRY?

With an understanding of what teacher inquiry is, how it contributes to professional growth, and how it differs from natural, daily reflection, let us consider the kinds of contexts that support teacher inquiry. As previously discussed, teaching is full of enormous complexities, paradoxes, and tensions, and hence, teaching itself invites inquiry. However, even as inquiry beckons each and every teacher, becoming a "lone inquirer" is difficult! For this reason, we explore three particularly ripe contexts for facilitating the development of an inquiry stance in practicing and prospective teachers—collegial study groups, student teaching and/or other clinical experiences, and professional development schools. You may currently be a part of one of these three contexts or you may wish to seek these contexts out as you begin and continue your teaching career.

Collegial Study Groups

Collegial study groups serve to connect and network groups of professionals together to do just what their name suggests—*study* practice. By their own nature, then, collegial study groups enhance the possibilities for conducting an inquiry and cultivating a community of inquirers. Critical Friends' Groups (CFGs) are one example of collegial study groups. The CFGs emerged out of the National School Reform Faculty's (NSRF) work, a professional development initiative that focuses on developing collegial relationships, encouraging reflective practice, and rethinking leadership in restructuring schools. The CFGs provide deliberate time and structures dedicated to promoting adult professional growth that is directly linked to student learning. In addition to the CFGs advocated by the NSRF, the Southern Maine Partnership also provides protocols and frameworks for not only developing inquiry skills but also nurturing the development of professional learning communities. More information regarding the creation of critical friends groups and professional learning communities can be found on the following Web sites: http://www.harmonyschool.org/nsrf/default.html and http://www.usm.maine.edu/smp/about/index.html. Creating collegial study groups facilitates the development of a professional learning community within your school. When you join a collegial study group or community of inquirers, your collaborative investigation into shared goals begins and your odds of achieving those goals become greatly enhanced.

Student Teaching and/or Other Clinical Experiences

If you are a veteran teacher, you likely reminisce about your own student teaching experience as an important feature of your preservice education. Similarly, if you are a prospective teacher, you have likely looked forward to your field experience and student teaching with great anticipation. According to a research report prepared by the U.S. Department of Education and the Office for Educational Research Improvement,

Learning to teach typically involves spending considerable time in schools participating in field experiences of varying lengths, the staples of teacher preparation programs. Study after study shows that experienced and newly certified teachers alike see clinical experiences (including student teaching) as a powerful—sometimes the single most powerful—component of teacher preparation.

Whether that power enhances the quality of teacher preparation, however, may depend on the specific characteristics of the field experience. (Wilson, Floden, & Ferrini-Mundy, 2001, p. 17)

Mounting evidence suggests that field experiences that include engagement in teacher inquiry enhance the quality of teacher preparation (see, e.g., Dana & Silva, 2001; Wilson et al., 2001). The reason for this is quite logical. Given that the act of teaching is an enormously complex endeavor, "learning to teach" in any simple, step-by-step, short period of time is impossible. As a preservice teacher, you are immersed in the complexities of teaching for the first time in clinical experiences. Immersion in this complexity naturally encourages engagement in inquiry, as questions about teaching, schools, and schooling abound. As you student teach, inquiry can help you learn to identify the complexities and problems inherent in teaching and tease these complexities apart to gain insights into your work with children. Given the comprehensive nature of teaching, identifying complexities and striving to understand them is a process that lasts an entire career. Engagement in teacher inquiry as an integral component of field preparation enhances the power of the field experiences. As you simultaneously learn to teach and to inquire into teaching, these two processes become intricately intertwined. When teaching and inquiry become synonymous, you have cultivated an inquiry stance toward teaching that will serve you, your students, and the field of education well for the duration of your career!

Professional Development Schools

Since the late 1980s, a specialized setting for student teaching and other field experiences has emerged—professional development schools (PDSs). According to Darling-Hammond (1994), professional development schools

aim to provide new models of teacher education and development by serving as exemplars of practice, builders of knowledge, and vehicles for communicating professional understanding among teacher educators, novices, and veteran teachers. They support the learning of prospective and beginning teachers by creating settings in which novices enter professional practice by working with expert practitioners, enabling veteran teachers to renew their own professional development and assume new roles as mentors, university adjuncts, and teacher leaders. They allow school and university educators to engage jointly in research and rethinking of practice, thus creating an opportunity for the profession to expand its knowledge base by putting research into practice—and practice into research. (p. 1)

Professional development schools grew out of Goodlad's *Teachers for Our Nation's Schools* (1990) and *Tomorrow's Teachers: A Report of the Holmes Group* (Holmes Group, 1986). *Tomorrow's Teachers* was written by the Holmes Group, "a consortium of education deans and chief academic officers from the major research universities in each of the fifty states" (p. 3). Their primary purpose was to come together as a group to improve the quality of their teacher education programs. Although The Holmes Group (1986) has evolved significantly since the mid-1980s, one of the original goals of the group is still strong:

> If university faculties are to become more expert educators of teachers, they must make better use of expert teachers in the education of other teachers and in research on teaching. In addition, schools must become places where both teachers and university faculty can systematically inquire into practice and improve it. (p. 4)

This goal from the original Holmes Group publication clearly notes the importance of systematic inquiry in the PDS. The Holmes Group has evolved to become The Holmes Partnership, where public schools and universities apply for a joint membership in the organization. If you are a practicing or prospective teacher in a PDS, your school and university may be a member of this growing organization that promotes teacher inquiry.

In an inquiry-oriented professional development school, teacher inquiry is a central part of the professional practice of all members of the PDS—practicing teachers, prospective teachers, administrators, and university teacher educators. This transition to inquiry is the mechanism for reinventing schools as "learning" organizations. Hence, a PDS culture supports and celebrates the engagement of teachers and other PDS professionals in constructing knowledge through intentional, systematic inquiry and using that knowledge to continually reform, refine, and change the practice of teaching.

HOW DOES MY ENGAGING IN TEACHER INQUIRY HELP SHAPE THE PROFESSION OF TEACHING?

Regardless of your method of inquiry, the subject of your inquiry, or the context of your inquiry, what is most important is that you *do* inquire!

According to numerous leading scholars on teaching and teacher education, such as Aronowitz and Giroux (1985), Greene (1986), and Zeichner (1986), "teachers are decision makers and collaborators who must reclaim their roles in the shaping of practice by taking a stand as both educators and activists" (Cochran-Smith, 1991, p. 280). Inquiry is a core tool teachers evoke when making informed and systematic decisions. Through the inquiry process, teachers can support with evidence the decisions they make as educators and, subsequently, advocate for particular children changes in curriculum and/or changes in pedagogy. Inquiry ultimately emerges as action and results in change.

As a prospective teacher, practicing teacher, or mentor-teacher interested in problematizing your professional practice, you have committed to simultaneous renewal and reform of the teaching profession and teacher education! Teacher inquiry is the ticket to enact this reform! Cochran-Smith and Lytle (1993) claim that in any classroom where teacher inquiry is occurring, "there is a radical, but quiet kind of educational reform in process" (p. 101). Your individual engagement in teacher inquiry is a contribution to larger educational reform, a transformation of the teaching profession . . . so let us begin the journey!

The Start of Your Journey: Finding a Wondering 2

WHERE DO I BEGIN?

In Chapter 1, we welcomed you to teacher inquiry by defining the process, discussing inquiry as professional development, and exploring the relationship between inquiry and educational reform. This welcome to inquiry places you, as prospective and practicing teachers, in charge of your own professional growth and development. Leading your own learning is likely quite different from many of your past experiences in preservice and inservice teacher education. If you are a prospective teacher, up to this point you have likely engaged in coursework at college, where professors define learning objectives for you in course syllabi, choose your education texts, and define assignments that must be completed for graduation and initial certification. If you are a veteran teacher, you have likely attended inservice sessions covering topics that have been selected for you by administrators or curriculum specialists in your district or perhaps topics that are mandated by your state. Hence, by taking charge of your own learning, you are beginning your journey into uncharted territory! Charting new territory, when you are unfamiliar with both the terrain and your final destination, can be exciting but also quite frightening. Beginning your journey becomes less daunting after you do some initial preparation and take your first steps.

Just as hikers gather certain equipment before proceeding with a hike, as a teacher-inquirer you will need maps and a compass before you embark on your first inquiry journey. The map for this journey is what Kettering refers to as the welcoming attitude toward and active seeking of change: "Essentially research is nothing but a state of mind . . . a friendly, welcoming attitude toward change . . . going out to look for change instead of waiting for it to come" (Kettering, in Boyd, 1961). This welcoming attitude provides the foundation for mapping your inquiry journey. The compass that provides the direction or question for your inquiry comes from critical reflection in and on your own teaching practice.

As teachers seek out change and reflect on practice, the first step of their journey begins with brainstorming questions or wonderings for exploration. One teacher-inquirer describes the new stance she assumed toward her teaching as she prepared to begin her inquiry journey as follows:

> A teacher-inquirer is someone who searches for questions as well as answers. I am learning that saying, "I don't know" is not an admittance of failure, but a precursor of positive change. I have become comfortable with the expressions: "I wonder . . ." "I think . . . ," and "What if . . . ?" (Stiles, 1999)

WHERE DO I FIND MY WONDERINGS AND QUESTIONS?

A teacher's completion of the expressions "I wonder . . . ," "I think . . . ," and "What if . . . ?" do not materialize out of thin air. According to Hubbard and Power (1993), teachers' wonderings and questions come from their "real-world observations and dilemmas" (p. 2). After working with hundreds of teacher researchers, we believe that a teacher's wonderings materialize as professional passions at the nexus of a teacher's work, his or her teaching dilemmas or "felt difficulties" (see Figure 2.1).

The complex nature of teaching makes the profession an especially ripe context for cultivating an inquiry question. Teaching requires teachers to make sense of the interaction between the following five elements simultaneously: *the child, the context, the content, the acts of teaching,* and *the teacher's own beliefs or dispositions.* So how do teachers think about the five elements of teacher work? In any teaching event, teachers consider the *context* where they teach. For instance, they may ponder, "What resources are available?", "What are the state standards or system objectives?", "What support is provided for this innovation?", or, "How will the broader community react?" In conjunction with thinking about context, teachers also make sure that they understand the key *content* knowledge that must be constructed. Teachers ask, "What misinformation or misunderstandings often occur as children construct knowledge in this area?" and "What are the multiple perspectives that must be shared in order to capture the complexity of the content?"

In addition to recognizing the impact of the context and the key underpinnings of the content that must be taught, teachers consider *the children* whom they will need to teach. They raise questions such as, "Who will need more scaffolding?", "How can I make this content relevant to my students?", and, "How can I accommodate the diverse learners within my classroom?" All of these areas and questions influence the acts of teaching. For example, as teachers determine which curriculum and content are relevant, they plan, select, and use instructional strategies. They also identify assessment tools that will support student learning. Teacher decision making is even further complicated by the presence of a *teacher's beliefs* and professional identity. Teachers may wonder, "How do my own attitudes toward writing influence my teaching?" or, "How do my beliefs about learning influence the way I accommodate diverse learners?" These five elements are central to teachers' thinking and provide the foundation for identifying felt difficulties or teaching dilemmas that prompt the development of inquiry questions.

Qualitative researcher Robert Sherman (1997) argues that powerful research questions emerge from "felt difficulties." Teachers are constantly faced with "felt difficulties" or dilemmas as they reflect in and on their acts of teaching. As a result, these "felt difficulties" are direct concerns that emerge from one's own teaching experiences. Figure 2.1 presents how these five elements representing the complexity of teaching and the resulting dilemmas or "felt difficulties" of teaching merge to form eight passions.

In this chapter, we map out the eight passions that emerged from our analysis of over 100 teacher inquiries. In some ways, each of the eight passions overlaps with each other, but we present them as distinct entities in order to help you view an array of possibilities for finding and defining your first wondering. Each passion is illustrated with the work of one or more teacher-inquirers. As we share excerpts from the work of these prospective and practicing teachers, we analyze the thought processes they utilized to derive their first wondering. In so doing, we offer you practical suggestions and guidance as you progress through a similar process. Finally, we end each section with exercises designed to help you explore areas that are ripe for the development of your wonderings. You may wish to pause at the end of each section to complete these exercises before reading farther. By the end of this chapter, we hope you will have defined a question to get you started and can celebrate the completion of what is often the most difficult component of teacher inquiry—defining your question and getting started.

Passion 1: Helping an Individual Child

You are likely familiar with a very common saying proudly displayed by many teachers:

Figure 2.1

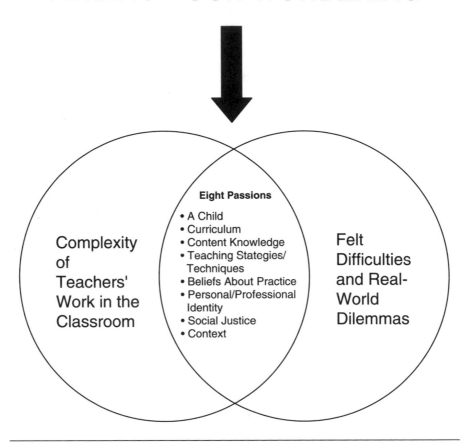

FINDING YOUR WONDERING

Eight Passions

- A Child
- Curriculum
- Content Knowledge
- Teaching Stategies/ Techniques
- Beliefs About Practice
- Personal/Professional Identity
- Social Justice
- Context

Complexity of Teachers' Work in the Classroom

Felt Difficulties and Real-World Dilemmas

A hundred years from now, it will not matter what my bank account was, the sort of house I lived in, or the kind of car I drove. But the world may be different because I was important in the life of a child.

In fact, you may have very well entered the teaching profession on the basis of your passion for children, your talent for connecting with them, and your willingness to commit yourself to touching children's lives.

Each year, classroom teachers encounter particular learners who stand out from the rest for a variety of reasons—perhaps a learner is struggling with a particular concept in the curriculum, is experiencing difficulty in social interactions, has progressed far beyond the expectations for your particular grade level and is in need of enrichment, or behaves in ways that are not conducive to your classroom learning environment. These learners are like puzzles that teachers try to understand as they strive to make a difference in a particular child's life.

A puzzling child can be a wonderful source for sparking your first wondering. If you are a beginning teacher, this is a common, comfortable, and developmentally appropriate place to develop your inquiry stance toward teaching. If you are a practicing teacher, you may also find that studying a particular student can contribute to and facilitate the child's experience in your classroom, the Individualized Education Plan (IEP) or staffing process within your school, as well as inform your own ability to accommodate individual differences and track student growth. Each year, we work with numerous prospective and practicing teachers who use the process of inquiry to gain insights into learners who stand out to them in their classrooms. A few examples follow.

Amy Ruth, an intern in a kindergarten classroom, did not have a difficult time generating a large number of curiosities and wonderings for her first inquiry project. In fact, Amy ended each of her professional journal entries with questions that emerged from her daily practice. As she brainstormed, she came to the realization that many of her wonderings focused on student growth, and she eventually narrowed her inquiry to focus on an English as a Second Language (ESL) learner in her classroom. As you read the following excerpt from Amy's inquiry, note how she describes the process of finding her wondering:

> It was not hard for me to come up with a huge number of curiosities or wonderings that I have within my classroom. As I began to narrow down the wonderings, I began noticing that many of them centered around topics that held things in common, particularly the following areas: peer interactions, peer influence, ESL students, and the kindergarten writing center. Out of the list that I narrowed down, I asked myself, "What is it that really fascinates me?", "What am I passionate about?", and, "Why am I a teacher?" The answer to all three of these questions for me is *student growth*. It fascinates me to see the enormous growth students have over a period of time. I am passionate about setting up a learning environment that fosters growth. I am a teacher because it is the challenge of finding ways to help a child grow, the excitement in the student growth as it is taking place, and the joy I feel of seeing that growth has and is taking place within my classroom!

My inquiry project became more apparent as I began to take over at the writing center during Language Arts time. Since the beginning of the year, I had watched one ESL student's language develop and grow right before my eyes. His forceful nature, strong personality, and undying energy, had at times exhausted me, while at the same time empowered me. He instilled a challenge in me to find ways to facilitate his entrance into our school, our classroom community, and our language. For being a child who came to school knowing very little of the English language, he is extremely outgoing and eager to be accepted by his teachers and his peers.

It was not long after I began working with the students at the writing center that I decided that my inquiry would focus on this ESL student, who I will refer to as Adam. As an intern in a kindergarten classroom, from the beginning of the year I had been amazed by the growth students show in their illustrating and drawing. I am always full of wonder and amazement as children's one-page illustrations develop into seven- or eight-page detailed stories.

The first time that Adam's group came to the writing center, I was "blown away" to see how he interacted with his peers. Immediately after sitting down with his writing folder, he handed a new sheet of paper to a peer, Kevin, and told him to draw a fish. "Fish!" he said. "Big Fish!" I was amazed at the request. The thought that Adam would ask Kevin, a well-known artist in our room, seemed so clever to me. Where would this request lead Adam in his writing? Was this interaction/request going to be typical of Adam at the writing center? Would this help Adam's written language develop, as his spoken language had recently?

Now I had found my initial inquiry wondering: How does peer interaction facilitate Adam's writing at the kindergarten writing center? (Ruth, 1999)

To find her first wondering, Amy began by raising questions as she journaled about her classroom each day. Then, she began listing broad categories of areas that fascinated her—peer interactions, ESL students, the writing process. She found a common theme that connected all of her current fascinations in her teaching—student growth. Finally, an observation of an interaction between two of her learners during a writer's workshop triggered the final focus of her inquiry wondering. This incident provides a fine illustration of what Hubbard and Power refer to as inquiry resulting from "real-world observations."

Wonderings also come from "dilemmas" or "felt difficulties." In the next example, note how Quinn Garmen encountered a very common dilemma faced by many beginning teachers—she actually began to fear a student who challenged her directions:

> Imagine that you are a prestudent teacher in a kindergarten room during the third day of your experience. At her request, all of the students join your cooperating teacher on the rug for a story . . . all except one child, "Suzy." After I remind Suzy several times that it is time to stop her project and join the others on the rug, she continues to color using just one more marker, to sprinkle glitter in just one more place, and to put on just one more piece of sequin. Then, instead of quietly joining the group, she decides it would be more exciting to also sprinkle glitter on the work table, pour glue on the carpet, and use marker wherever there is room on the floor, the table, and even her hands. The more she ignores my reminders, the more frustrated and agitated I become. Finally, with a stern face and voice, I stoop down to Suzy's eye level and give her a choice: Either she can quietly meet Mrs. Brown and the others at the rug or she can have a time-out. Just as those seemingly harmless words spill off the tip of my tongue, Suzy raises her right hand and with all her might, grazes my cheek with a mixture of pure anger and fear while yelling, "no!" Her unexpected reaction immediately stuns my words and freezes me like a popsicle. My numb legs can barely hold my paralyzed body up straight. Unaware of the situation, Mrs. Brown gently reminds Suzy that her place is at the rug. Immediately, Suzy bolts from the scene and finds a cozy spot right in front of the story, as if there from the start. For a few minutes afterwards, I can't move or think. I stand in a daze wondering what has just happened. Is this how this innocent five-year-old usually reacts to situations? Or is this just her way of reaching out?

> Unfortunately, this was not just an imagined scenario for me, but rather a serious "slap in the face." As absurd as this may sound, I actually began to fear Suzy. She was the first person I thought of in the morning and the last person I thought of at night. In fact, I found myself trying to avoid contact with her whenever possible. As horrible as this may sound, I sometimes felt more comfortable

working with someone who I knew would not hurt me rather than risk having a confrontation with Suzy. With all of this happening, I knew that I needed to develop a better relationship with Suzy during my student-teaching experience.

During this time, I began attending seminars on teacher inquiry and reading books on teacher research during my student teaching. This led me to question my own teaching beliefs and practices. This skepticism about my teaching, coupled with Suzy's slap, led me to complete a systematic study of our relationship. Therefore, the purpose of my study was to understand the behavioral patterns of one student, Suzy, in relation to my behavior as the teacher. The following research question guided my inquiry, "How do the structure and management of my classroom encourage or deter a particular student's behavior?" (Garman, 1997, pp. 1-4)

Like Amy, Quinn's question was triggered by a specific incident in the classroom that led her to focus on a particular child. In contrast to Amy's critical incident, where she observed two learners interacting with each other, Quinn's critical incident was characterized by her own interaction with a learner. Out of this particular interaction a dilemma developed—a desire to avoid a five-year-old whom she was responsible for teaching each day. Her wondering or "felt difficulty" was born out of the combination of her own interaction with a learner, subsequent reflection on that interaction, and desire to confront the dilemma she faced.

While you, like Amy and Quinn, note observations of particular learners and interact with individual learners hundreds of times each teaching day, sometimes a wondering about a particular child is not spawned by one observation or critical incident, but emerges from what you notice and are learning about a particular child over time. In this last example, note how Jenn Thulin's (1999) interest in a particular first-grade child emerged after many months of discussion and observation between Jenn and her mentor-teacher:

Meg is an imaginative child who stood out to my mentor-teacher and I from the beginning of the year when she told us her stories of castles, princesses, and dogs that talk. She told these stories with the enthusiasm and excitement of an actress who was "on stage." We knew that she was very creative, but did not know the extent of her talent until she sang to us one day. Meg sang with the most incredible voice and perfect pitch. She not only enjoyed singing songs but also making up her own songs as well.

While it was clear from the first day of school that Meg was a very talented and creative young girl, she also stood out in the classroom because of extreme language difficulties. At first we noticed problems with her speech. Many of her syllables were reversed and she would often substitute incorrect sounds. For example, she would say "bery" instead of "very." She also had a hard time processing auditory information such as questions and directions. From the beginning of the year Meg also struggled with all subjects, but was especially discouraged and falling behind in reading.

In contrast to most of her peers, she did not know many sounds and confused many letters of the alphabet. We struggled for many months to help her learn the alphabet and sounds. She would make progress, but it was inconsistent. Just because Meg knew a sound one day did not automatically guarantee she would know it the next day. To help her achieve consistency, it was necessary to give Meg a great deal of individual instruction.

Therefore, Meg was recommended as a candidate for Instructional Support, which led to observation and testing by a team of educators. Through this process, we discovered that Meg had very poor auditory processing skills and auditory memory. It was very hard for her to comprehend and remember things that were told to her orally. Meg scored extremely low on auditory processing; however, she scored exceptionally high in visual processing. If Meg saw a picture or a visual representation it was easy for her to understand. Because of the processing and memory difficulties, reading was a challenge for Meg. If you read Meg a passage from a book, she may not understand a word of it. However, if you showed her an illustration associated with that passage, she could tell you what the passage was about.

After witnessing the Instructional Support Process and observing Meg struggle throughout the year with reading, I wanted to find a way to help her. The first thing that came to my mind was music. I noticed not only that Meg was a wonderful singer but also that she remembered songs very easily, so I hoped that music might work well with her auditory memory and processing difficulties. I hoped there was some way I could connect music to reading. I wondered, "In what ways could I utilize music to help Meg become a better reader?" and "How might music help her combat some frustrations when reading and boost her self esteem?" (Thulin, 1999)

Jenn's long-term commitment to understanding and supporting an individual child provides a fertile foundation for the cultivation of this inquiry.

As you can see by looking across these three examples of inquiry into a particular child, inquiry questions emerge in a variety of ways.

Passion 1 Exercises

1. Create a list of all of the children in your class. As you add each child's name to the list, think about what makes that particular child unique. Jot down one question next to each child's name that would provide you with insights into this particular learner.

2. Thinking back over the course of the school year, create a "Top 10" list of critical incidents or intriguing observations that have occurred with particular learners in your classroom. Create a chart by generating a column next to each critical incident or observation that notes the child or children who were involved. Finally, in a third column, add a few words that describe the essence of the experience or observation. After you have completed your chart, look for themes across incidents, such as, "Does one child appear on my chart consistently?" and, "What are the commonalities between each of the incidents or observations I listed?"

Passion 2: Desire to Improve or Enrich Curriculum

Just as you are involved each day interacting with and observing children, each day of teaching you interact with the required curriculum that you are expected to teach. You work diligently to develop lessons and units of study that engage your children with meaningful content designed to actualize your objectives. Sometimes, for different reasons, teachers become dissatisfied with a curriculum unit and particular lessons that they have delivered in the past.

Locating your inquiry within the development or enrichment of curriculum is a ripe area for the development of your first wondering. A curriculum development inquiry is a popular form of inquiry for veteran teachers, as they often emerge from a dissatisfaction of "what was" the last time the unit was taught. In addition, veterans can reap the benefits of revising and enriching curriculum when they return to the same units or lessons each year. Inquiry into student learning as a result of teaching a particular "chunk" of curriculum can also provide the point of entry for inquiry for prospective teachers. This kind of inquiry allows prospective teachers to systematically explore and critique existing curriculum that can lead to changes in their own use of or conception of curriculum. Prospective teachers often teach curriculum for the first time in their field experience and study what student learning occurred as a result of the curriculum.

We now share two excerpts of veteran teacher inquiries motivated by the desire to improve curriculum. Judi Kur, a first-grade teacher, finds her initial wondering in the tension between the required teaching of an outdated dinosaur curriculum unit, focused on the acquisition of facts, and the specific topic that is highly motivating for her primary school-age children:

> I first thought about my inquiry project about the same time I began contemplating my upcoming responsibilities as the Chair of a unit entitled: Prehistoric Life and Fossils. In my district, teachers are organized into teams that collaborate to teach four thematic, literature-based units each school year. As the Unit Chair, it was my responsibility to organize activities, orchestrate the sharing of books and materials among the teachers on my team, and lead the development of a culminating activity at the close of the unit.
>
> I had been dissatisfied with most of the science units in the primary curriculum since I began teaching first grade in 1996. I enjoy science and am fascinated with teaching science. However, to me science curriculum should focus on topics that children can experiment with, topics where the students can use the scientific process to ask and answer questions. This had not been my experience with the dinosaur unit. Yes, the children love the topic and they are motivated to learn, but I didn't feel that I was taking advantage of the children's and my enthusiasm. This unit as it

was written didn't help me. In addition, a survey of the primary teachers in the district showed that most teachers thought the unit was extremely outdated. The science curriculum focuses on fossils, and the objectives can be covered in about a week, and to top it off, we were being told that we cannot use the word "theories" in our teaching of the unit, due to concerns expressed by parents that the dinosaur unit was teaching evolution and this was contrary to their religious beliefs.

Is it any wonder that when I last taught the dinosaur unit, the learning the children did was reading about other people's discoveries, not making their own? My students, as those mentioned by Craig Munsart in his book *Investigating Science with Dinosaurs* (1993) "easily memorized names and dimensions of dinosaurs but learned little about the science that surrounds them." And yet I agreed with a statement that I read by Don Lessem in an article in the *New York Times* (1991): "Dinosaurs are often a child's first introduction to science. As such, they could be the key to engendering a lifelong interest in all science."

And so, I wondered, "How can I take a science unit that is heavy on content, and make it more science inquiry based?" After reading the book *Organizing Wonder: Making Inquiry Science Work in the Elementary School* (1998) by Jody Hall and talking with Carla Zembal-Saul, a professor in science education at the university, I embarked on developing lessons for this unit framed around the question, "How do scientists know so much about dinosaurs?" Once my lessons were developed and implemented, I pondered an additional research question: "What evidence exists that my newly developed inquiry based lessons on dinosaurs help children develop the abilities advocated by the National Science Standards in the section that discusses science as inquiry?" (Kur, 2000)

In sum, Judi's inquiry question emerges from her dissatisfaction with existing curriculum and her own commitment to providing primary grade students the opportunity to experience scientific inquiry. As a result of these interacting conditions (students, curriculum, and teacher beliefs), Judi seeks outside support in the form of human and other resources to further refine her question.

Like Judi, fourth grade teaching colleagues Diane Reed and Amy Jones collaborated on an inquiry, finding their first wondering in a social studies unit on explorers. As you read the excerpt from Amy and Diane's inquiry, note that, once again, they articulate a dilemma or "felt difficulty" in the curriculum's existing approach to teaching about Columbus:

> "In 1492, Columbus sailed the ocean blue." Most elementary students early in their education learn this traditional verse. A less familiar verse, which comes to us from Native peoples, is "In 1493, Columbus stole all that he could see." This striking difference between the two quotes offers a glimpse at the task that we, as educators, are trying to accomplish by meshing two different perspectives in the teaching of the "true discovery" of America. This idea led to our collaboration, as two fourth-grade teachers, to investigate other possibilities for teaching a unit on Explorers in our district.
>
> Teaching the Explorer Unit presented several dilemmas that needed to be addressed prior to the implementation of the unit. First, we struggled with the fact that we had four weeks to instruct the children with the material. The question was raised, should we spend the four weeks highlighting several explorers, or should we focus on Columbus and do an in-depth study of his encounter with the native people?
>
> After reviewing the materials and discussing the time limitations together, we felt that our time and our students' time were better served by focusing on Columbus's encounter. With that decided, the next dilemma revolved around the concern of whether fourth-grade students are able to look at multiple perspectives and accuracy of historical events? This question initiated our framework for our inquiry.
>
> When we began working on this project, we first had to find our focal point. In *Rethinking Columbus* (Bigelow & Peterson, 1998), we found the following quote that would navigate our curriculum writing:
>
> 'Our goal is not to idealize native people, demonize Europeans, or present a depressing litany of victimization. We hope to encourage a deeper understanding of the European invasion's consequences, to honor the rich legacy of resistance to the injustices it created, to convey some appreciation for the diverse indigenous cultures of the hemisphere, and to reflect on what this all means for us today.' (p. 11)

We also needed to enhance our own background knowledge of this historical event. *Lies My Teacher Told Me: Everything Your American History Textbook Got Wrong* (Loewen, 1995) presented a more historically accurate account of Columbus's arrival. *The Tainos: The People Who Welcomed Columbus* (Jacobs, 1992) provided specific information on the lifestyle of the Tainos, both before and after the arrival of Columbus. Both resources were not developmentally appropriate for fourth graders; however, they provided us with the essential background knowledge needed to teach this unit.

As we began to review the literature for the unit, as well as additional resources, several questions emerged that became the basis for our inquiry project: "How can the story of the 'true discovery' of America be taught to fourth graders in a developmentally appropriate way?" and "What changes occur in students' knowledge/understanding of the 'true discovery' of America as a result of the lessons we constructed?"

Subquestions targeted at change emerged and included "What changes occur in students' knowledge/understanding of Columbus?", "What changes occur in students' knowledge/ understanding of the Taino people?", "What changes occur in students' knowledge/understanding of author's bias regarding the depiction of this historical event?", and "What changes occur in students' knowledge/understanding of the meaning of 'discovery'." (Jones & Reed, 2000)

Often, when teachers engage in inquiry around curriculum, they start with a "How can I?" phrased question. In Judi's case, she began with, "How can I take a science unit that is heavy on content and make it more inquiry based?" Similarly, in Amy and Diane's case, they began with, "How can we teach the story of the 'true discovery' of America to fourth graders in a developmentally appropriate way?" While "How can I . . ." phrased questions are wonderful starting points for curriculum development inquiries, if a teacher-inquirer stops here, his or her work may become purely the development of lesson plans without systematic study. While the development of new lesson plans and implementing these plans is important work, focusing on what is learned as a result of the curriculum development makes the work teacher inquiry. Hence, if you begin with a "How can I . . ." wondering, also formulate a companion wondering that leads you beyond the lessons you developed to what you have learned about children, curriculum, and/or yourself as a teacher as a result of developing and implementing these new lessons. These companion questions are often generated by engaging in adult-level research about the content as well as the teaching strategies you are about to use. In the examples above, Judi turned to Hall's (1998) *Organizing Wonder: Making Inquiry Science Work in the Elementary School*, whereas Amy and Diane read *Lies My Teacher Told Me: Everything Your American History Textbook Got Wrong* (Loewen, 1995) and *The Tainos: The People Who Welcomed Columbus* (Jacobs, 1992). In this case, content area reading becomes an essential component of wondering development.

Passion 2 Exercises

1. Browse through your textbooks, district's curriculum documents, and your old plan books. As you browse, generate a list of the topics you teach each school year that you felt uncomfortable teaching in the past or wished to enrich in some way. Next to each entry on your list, jot down a few words that describe your dissatisfaction with this unit and/or the ways the unit might be enhanced. Select one item from your list to focus a potential inquiry on, and begin the process of brainstorming questions related to the teaching of this curriculum.

2. Visit the Web sites of the leading national organizations for the teaching of subject matter, such as National Council for Teachers of Mathematics (www.nctm.org), National Science Teachers Association (www.nsta.org), National Council for the Social Studies (www.ncss.org), and National Council for Teachers of English (www.ncte.org). View each organization's standards for best practice in that field. How does the delivery of your curriculum mesh with best teaching practice as advocated by these associations?

3. Meet with the curriculum specialist or administrator in your building. Find out what changes they are anticipating in the curriculum. Identify an interest area and question connected to these changes. By studying the new implementation or change process, you are likely to have some influence regarding what develops!

Passion 3: Focus on
Developing Content Knowledge

In Passion 2, inquiry focused on developing curriculum with new alternative instructional approaches and objectives to shape curriculum. As indicated in both inquiries, a precursor to this kind of curriculum development was a focus on developing deeper teacher content knowledge and then identifying the developmentally appropriate content knowledge for the children within each teacher's classroom. In this case, the inquiry wondering emerges as teachers identify areas of the curriculum they teach that provoke a content-related "felt difficulty." For example, Diane and Amy's inquiry into "How can we teach the story of the 'true discovery' of America to fourth graders in a developmentally appropriate way?" provoked them to inquire into the underlying content of the curriculum they were planning. They needed to understand the voices represented in alternative stories. This required substantive adult-level content reading and research.

Inquiry or research into content requires multiple phases of teacher activity. First, the inquiry begins as teachers pose a question about the content they are teaching, for example, "What do I know about the 'true discovery' of America?", "What do I know about the Holocaust?", or "How do airplanes fly?" Next, teachers obtain multiple resources and perspectives that can help them respond to that inquiry. For example, teachers may explore reference materials, review primary documents, conduct an oral history, or delve into artifacts that inform their inquiry question. One teacher shared the following:

> You know, as an elementary teacher, I really don't have the time to be an expert on anything. I felt really fortunate to have the time to investigate one content area in depth and figure out a way to make sense of it for my young students. The Holocaust is a particularly sensitive issue. I am always wondering what my first through fourth graders should know about it and what I can teach them that is really at their level of understanding. After spending a good month reading everything that I could about the Holocaust and really trying to get an adult-level understanding of the events and atrocities that happened, I finally felt prepared to teach. (Fieldnotes, SBAC Teacher)

By exploring multiple sources, the teacher constructs a stronger understanding of the various perspectives on the content she needs to teach.

Once the adult-level content knowledge has been developed, teachers begin the third step of the inquiry, which focuses on defining what is believed to be the developmentally appropriate content for the students within the classroom. This is a "teacher activity" since it requires teachers to investigate their own students' cognitive, physical, social, and emotional levels regarding the content area investigated. One example of this emerged as elementary teachers considered the students' readiness for the content of the Holocaust as follows:

> We talked to a lot of people about how to share the Holocaust with young children. We spoke to our administrator, guidance counselor, and a slew of parents. We met with the media specialist, too, and some local experts on the Holocaust. We even talked to members of the Jewish Community within our town. I think the most important information came from interviews with our students. Although most of them knew nothing about the Holocaust themselves, which wasn't surprising to us, we realized through analyzing our data that certain content specific to the Holocaust should be incorporated into the elementary curriculum and that, in addition, certain democratic dispositions or underpinnings for addressing and understanding issues of the Holocaust were missing from our current curriculum. (Fieldnotes, SBAC Teacher)

After a great deal of background research, this elementary teacher and her inquiry partner decided that it was more developmentally appropriate to structure the elementary students' learning around key ideas underpinning the Holocaust as follows:

> By the time we finished digging into our own understanding of the Holocaust, we realized that our students needed to understand some fundamental ideas. We focused on helping our students develop themselves in moral and responsible ways by promoting a caring and accepting nature toward others. We taught them the importance of helping others seek better conditions and the difference between being a "bystander" and a "rescuer." We focused on teaching them about "random acts of kindness," developing good habits, and respecting "otherness." We also worked on helping our students understand that change is necessary in the world if we are to survive and that prejudice, discrimination, and stereotyping are unproductive activities if we strive to reach these goal. (Fieldnotes, SBAC Teacher)

Interestingly, these teachers decided that these were the important concepts for their students to learn in regard to the content of the Holocaust.

Since the teacher is key to student learning, spending your time constructing content knowledge and transforming that knowledge into developmentally appropriate content for children is a legitimate and worthy task. You will not only become much more familiar with the content, but you will also become more clear about what you do not know. Exploring content and determining its relevance to the students within your classroom is a powerful way to enhance your teaching and the learning process.

Passion 3 Exercises

1. Make a list of topics you teach that you believe would enhance your classroom practice if you possessed deeper content knowledge. On this list, circle the topics that you believe require substantive transformation or adaptation if you are to teach the content area to children.

2. Evaluate the materials you currently use to teach content within each subject area and unit you teach. Do these resources represent diversity of perspectives and multiple voices? Whose voices are present or missing?

Passion 4: Desire to Improve or Experiment With Teaching Strategies and Teaching Techniques

In Passions 2 and 3, wonderings are located around a particular topic and content area. The work of the teacher also encompasses applying generic teaching strategies (such as cooperative learning, role play, simulation, lecture, and discussion), as well as specific teaching techniques (such as questioning, assessing student learning, and integrating technology into instruction), throughout the teaching day. Similar to the desire to improve or enhance a particular piece of curriculum as discussed in Passion 2, you may have a desire to gain insights into, improve, and/or experiment with new or routine teaching strategies and techniques. In the example below, Nancy Sunner is intrigued with learning more about the questions she poses to students in her daily teaching:

> Questioning is an enormously powerful and important skill in productive teaching. For decades, teacher questioning has been a topic of study. Researchers had found that teachers rely on questioning as an essential element of their teaching repertoire. On an average, elementary school teachers ask 348 questions during a typical school day (Acheson & Gall, 1997). Through the process of effective questioning, teachers can stimulate thought, help students reinforce basic skills, involve shy or quiet students, draw in the attention of a student who has drifted off, and promote self-esteem and success in the classroom.
>
> The skill of effective questioning requires teachers to constantly balance several things at once. During questioning, teachers must remember their lesson goals, monitor their communication with the students, assess the students' verbal and nonverbal responses (nods, raised hands, shrugs, and downcast eyes), and think about the next question. This impressive and sometimes overwhelming aspect of teaching sparked my curiosity about my own questioning techniques in the classroom.
>
> As a beginning teacher, I have experienced great satisfaction when I asked a student a question and I got a correct response. I feel as though the students "get it" and I am somehow responsible for this accomplishment. On the other hand, I have had experiences this year when a lesson is falling apart and it seems that no matter what questions are asked, the students cannot follow my line of questioning. This is the ultimate frustrating experience for everyone.
>
> Therefore, the focus of my inquiry is to better understand my questioning behavior as a teacher. The questions I will address through this inquiry are "What type of questions do I ask?" and "How does questioning change with the subjects I am teaching?" (Sunner, 1999)

Of the examples of teachers' wonderings we have explored thus far, note that Nancy's wonderings are perhaps the most straightforward and technical in nature. They emerge at the intersection of her professional readings and her "felt difficulty" regarding her use of questioning. Straightforward and technical wonderings are often powerful in that they lead to teachers' discoveries that their beliefs, philosophies, and desires are not always congruent with their practice. For example, through scripting the questions posed throughout different lessons and sorting each question into one of five categories (higher order/thought questions, recall/narrow questions, managerial/behavioral questions, procedural questions, and probing questions) as her inquiry unfolded, Nancy discovered that the majority of her questions were fact/recall questions. This discovery was inconsistent with her desire to teach for conceptual understanding and led to keener attention to her questioning efforts as well as changes in her questioning.

There is an old proverb, "A fish would be the last creature to discover water." In teaching, generic strategies and techniques can become so routine and ingrained in our practice that we do not notice significant ways our routines interface with the goals of our teaching. In addition, we can become so immersed in strategies and routines that have worked in the past that we fail to try new strategies that could potentially enhance our teaching. Systematically studying teaching strategies and techniques can lead to discoveries that would not have become apparent in the absence of systematic study, and these discoveries ultimately lead to new and significant change in teaching practice.

Passion 4 Exercises

1. Brainstorm a list of teaching strategies you would like to try. Next to each entry on your list, jot down a few words that describe your reasoning for wanting to try this strategy. Formulate a question that connects the strategy and your reasoning for trying using that strategy. For example:

   a. Cooperative Learning—My students are very talkative. Cooperative learning could fulfill their need to talk and focus their talking on academic learning simultaneously—How can I use my children's social skills to enhance their learning and instruction at the same time?

   b. Integrating a SMART Board into Instruction—After seeing a SMART Board demonstrated at a conference I recently attended, I was intrigued by the power this technology might hold to enhance instruction, but reluctant to try a SMART Board as my prior teaching experiences suggest that integrating technology into instruction can be intimidating and frustrating—How can a team of teachers work through problems together and support each other to overcome hurdles when using new technologies?

2. Brainstorm a list of the most frequent strategies and/or techniques you draw on in your teaching. After brainstorming your list, place a star next to the strategies that are most intriguing to you. Jot down a few sentences or phrases next to your starred strategies that capture why these techniques are intriguing. Then, formulate a question that connects the strategy and your intrigue with it. For example:

a. *Questioning—Sometimes children don't answer the questions I am asking—How do the ways I phrase questions contribute to how learners interpret them?

b. *Facilitating Discussions—During my literature circles, it feels like the children never talk to each other when discussing a book. The conversations feel like they resemble Ping–Pong matches as the dialog goes back and forth between me and my students: teacher→student→teacher→student→teacher→ student. I'd prefer the students to talk to each other. What are some strategies I could utilize to facilitate better literature discussions?

Passion 5: Desire to Explore the Relationship Between Your Beliefs and Your Classroom Practice

In the example used to illustrate Passion 4, Nancy's wondering led to her conclusion that her teaching desires and her practice were inconsistent with each other. While Nancy's inquiry *ended* with this discovery, many teachers *begin* their inquiry with the realization that the relationship between their beliefs and practice are incongruent. Exploring the relationship between your beliefs and practice provides another possibility for generating your first wondering.

In the example that follows, Holly Niebauer Jones finds her first teacher inquiry wondering as she discovers that her implementation of a classroom management plan does not match her philosophy:

I was fortunate to be a part of an experimental student teacher as researcher program at Penn State designed to focus on learning about and doing teacher research during the student teaching experience. Class discussions about teacher research and three books entitled *The Art of Classroom Inquiry* (1993) by Ruth Shagoury Hubbard and Brenda Miller Power, *Inside/Outside: Teacher Research and Knowledge* (1993) by Marilyn Cochran-Smith and Susan L. Lytle, and *Teachers as Researchers: Qualitative Inquiry as a Path to Empowerment* (1991) by Joe Kincheloe helped give me a strong background for pursuing research.

As I progressed through the semester, I thought of numerous projects that were possibilities for teacher research projects. The topic that consistently surfaced, however, was that I noticed inconsistencies between my philosophy of education and my actions as a teacher, particularly as they related to classroom management. The idealistic components in my philosophy were not always practiced. I pondered over this daily and wanted to find reasons for the inconsistencies.

In order to focus my data collection for research, I generated two questions: (1) In what ways do my classroom management and practices deter from my philosophy of teaching and my beliefs about how children learn? and (2) What are my underlying/ suppressed beliefs about teaching and learning and children and schooling that cause/contribute to the gaps that exist between my beliefs and my actions? (Niebauer, 1997)

As you can see, Holly found her inquiry at the intersection of her espoused teaching philosophy and her ability to critically self-reflect on her own classroom management.

Passion 5 Exercises

1. Write a series of philosophy statements that describe your general teaching philosophy; your philosophy of teaching science, social

studies, reading/language arts, mathematics; and/or creating a classroom learning environment conducive to instruction. (If you are a preservice teacher, you may have already completed essays such as these in your prior teacher preparation course-work at the university). Once committed to paper, share your philosophy with a colleague or friend. Discuss the ways you are and are not enacting your philosophies of teaching in your classroom practice.

2. Keep a teaching journal for one week. Each night, reflect on one happening in the classroom that you wish you had the opportunity to repeat and react to in a different way. Note what beliefs you hold that led you to react as you did, as well as how you would react differently if able to turn back time. What beliefs undergird your alternative reaction?

Passion 6: The Intersection of Your Personal and Professional Identities

Just as wonderings may be found at the intersection of your beliefs and practice, they may also be found at the intersection of your personal and professional identity. According to William Ayers (1989), who you are as a teacher and who you are as a person are intricately intertwined. In his study of six exemplary preschool teachers, he came to the conclusion that,

> "Teaching as identity" is the clearest theme to emerge in this inquiry, and "teaching as identity" is the frame through which each portrait makes sense. In these portraits, there is no clear line delineating the person and the teacher. Rather, there is a seamless web between teaching and being, between teacher and person. Teaching is not simply what one does, it is who one is. (p. 130)

Hence, a wonderful place to find your first wondering is by focusing on who you are as a person and a teacher and further exploring one of your own personal passions and the ways that passion plays out in your teaching.

An example of personal passion translating to teaching is found in the work of Julie Russell. In Julie's inquiry below, note how her personal passion for writing led to her first wonderings:

I can still remember every detail of the moment when I became a writer. The warm August air sticks to my skin, powdery chalk dust tickles my nose, and the comforting sounds of my mother making dinner fill my ears whenever I begin to put words on a page. I found my voice as a writer the summer before second grade. I was six years old, and my older sister had suddenly decided that she was too mature to play with me. She would disappear with her friends, and I was left to fill the long, summer days without her. One afternoon, I wandered into the basement and started to draw on an old chalkboard that my sister and I used when we were "playing school." After a while, I stopped drawing and began writing poetry. When my mother called me for dinner, she saw my poems and became my first audience. She encouraged my efforts and gave me a small, yellow notebook so I could continue to write. My passion for writing grew as I continued to read quality literature and experienced the powerful ways in which expert authors manipulate language and develop engaging stories. Throughout my life, I have turned to written words to express my thoughts and ideas.

As I developed a teaching philosophy, I realized that my passion for teaching is intertwined with my passion for writing. My goal as a teacher is to help children become lifelong learners who can think critically about the world around them and create and articulate their own ideas. I hope that, by sharing my love for writing with my students, I can help them express the thoughts and opinions that are important and meaningful to them. Therefore, when I pictured my future classroom, I always seemed to arrive during writer's workshop. I assumed that I would be an effective, engaging writing teacher simply because I enjoyed writing. I imagined a classroom filled with eager students who loved writing and could not wait to commit their ideas to paper. I was thrilled to be an intern in a second-grade classroom, because I could remember the wonderful writing experiences I had during my own second-grade year.

As I began my internship experience, I helped provide writing instruction for a group of second graders with differing strengths, needs, and interests. I quickly realized that teaching writing is extremely complicated. Some children wrote independently and produced several pages of text during each workshop. Others wrote one sentence at a time and frequently approached me to ask, "Am I done yet?" I often sat with a small group of students who struggled to get their thoughts down on paper. As I tried to keep these children on task and encourage them to continue writing, I asked questions and made story maps. At the end of many writing sessions, I felt uncomfortable with the amount of support I was giving to some young writers. Several children who were quite capable of writing independently often came to me and asked, "Can I write with you?" I worried that I was allowing some children to become too dependent on my help and my influence was hindering the flow of their ideas.

As I studied children's writing development, I realized that the range of writing behaviors in my classroom was common for second graders. I felt relief when I read the experts' descriptions of second-grade writers and they mirrored my feelings about the young writers in my classroom. Some children write "fluently" and approach writing with "carefree confidence" (Calkins, 1986, p. 67). These children write long, detailed narratives with ease. Other children seem to erase more than they write. Second graders are beginning to become "aware of an audience" for their writing, and the "easy confidence" they felt as first graders often turns into their first cases of "writer's block" (Calkins, 1986, p. 68). They are concerned about approaching tasks in the "right way" and that vulnerability makes writing a difficult and painstaking process for many children (Calkins, 1986, p. 69). Therefore, writing instruction in second grade must address this wide range of writing behaviors.

During the students' goal-setting conferences in the beginning of the school year, my mentor, Linda Witmer, spoke to many of the children about working toward meeting the district's benchmark for writing by the end of the year. According to this benchmark, the students must be able to write stories with beginnings, middles, and endings. These stories should be understandable and must include characters, settings, and major events. The students are also expected to include some descriptive language, use some punctuation and capitalization, and spell the district benchmark words correctly. The students must complete the writing assessment independently. After winter break, Linda and I were both concerned about our students' writing. As I looked through the students' work, I noticed that extremely capable children were often scoring below the benchmark. Many of the children were still writing incomplete stories, and endings were particularly difficult for many students. Although our students had wonderful, creative ideas, we worried that several of them would not meet the district's benchmark for writing because they did not take the reader on a complete journey from beginning to middle to end.

My initial experiences as a writing teacher were frustrating. After years of imagining myself as an effective writing teacher, I was dismayed when I realized that my efforts were not helping my students meet their writing goals. In some cases, I worried that I was doing more harm than good because my attempts to help often became persistent prompting that drowned out the students' voices in their own writing. I was heartbroken when students resisted writing, because I was so eager to share my passion for stories and language. When I conducted a survey to collect data about the students' attitudes toward writing, I was concerned when I realized that many children thought that they were good writers because of "neat handwriting," "good spelling," or "using time wisely." Although those skills are important, I noticed that most children did not mention that they were proud of their ability to create stories. Gradually, I began to doubt my ability to provide my students with writing instruction that would help them meet the district's writing goals and that would inspire them to enjoy writing. My passion for writing, which I believed would be an asset in the classroom, actually hindered my progress as a writing teacher because I struggled to relate to and communicate with students who resisted writing. As I studied writing instruction, I learned that a teacher's personal experiences with the subject matter influences the way he or she teaches his or her students (Frank, 1979). I realized that, because I had positive writing experiences as a child, I naively assumed that all of my second graders would react to writing with similar enthusiasm.

My passion for writing and teaching, as well as my frustrations about the realities of teaching writing, led me to my wonderings. I wanted to do a project that would focus on my students' development as writers and would also help me develop as a writing teacher. Therefore, I began my project with the following wonderings: "Will my second graders write more complete stories if the elements of a story are broken down into a series of mini-lessons?", "Will my second graders become more independent writers and gain confidence in their writing abilities if my expectations for their writing are more explicit?", "Will collaborating with other learners help my students grow as writers?", "Will my students grow as writers if the lessons include opportunities to make connections between children's literature and their own stories?", and "Will these changes in writing instruction improve the way my students feel about themselves as writers and the way I feel about myself as a writing teacher?" (Russell, 2002)

As indicated, Julie's wonderings developed from her own personal interest in writing and her identity as a writer. The exercises at the end of this section help you explore who you are as a person and teacher and serve as precursors to the development of wonderings that intersect your personal and professional identities.

> **Passion 6 Exercises**
>
> 1. Write your own autobiography. Discuss the development of your own interests and passions. Finally, discuss the factors that led to your chosen career field as a teacher.
>
> 2. Design a time line of your growth and development as a person and a teacher, beginning with your birth and noting years and dates of critical incidents that impacted your personal and professional life.
>
> 3. Follow the guide provided to design a Teacher's Coat of Arms. In space 1, draw a real or mythical animal that best describes the teacher you want to be. In space 2, choose a real symbol, or create your own design, for an insignia that best describes the teacher you want to be. In space 3, choose one color in any shade—or a rainbow effect that best describes the teacher you want to be. In space 4, draw one character, real or fictional, that best describes the teacher you want to be. In space 6, choose one word that best describes the teacher you want to be. How you write that word should also help to describe the teacher you want to be.

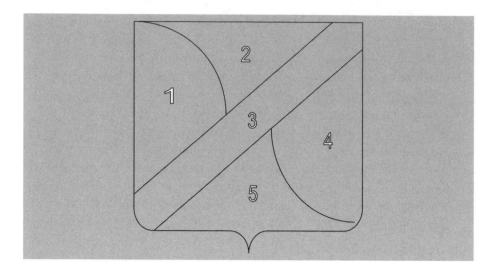

Passion 7: Advocating Social Justice

Recall from Chapter 1 the notion that engaging in inquiry is a responsibility you accept as a teacher that enables you to take a stand and effect educational change. By generating data and evidence to support the decisions and positions you take as an educator, reform in classrooms and schools can result in the promotion of social justice. According to Cochran-Smith and Lytle (1993),

> When teachers research their own practice . . . they begin to envision alternative configurations of human and material resources to meet the needs of culturally diverse groups of students, teachers, and administrators. And they are willing to invest more of their own resources and professional energy in larger efforts to reform classrooms and schools. (p. 80)

Your first teacher inquiry wondering may come from your desire to effect social change by exploring questions of race, class, gender, or disability. In fact, effecting social change in regard to issues of social justice may indeed become the focus for your entire teaching career. Inquiry can be a powerful vehicle that begins your journey working toward this goal.

In the example below, teaching intern Andrea Hosfeld begins her journey toward exploring questions related to teaching for social justice:

As a child growing up in the 1980s, I believed that the world was a place where anyone with an aspiration could succeed with determination. It was a time when poverty and racism were covered by a thick haze of Reaganite rhetoric. Men and women of every race and nationality need only believe that their dreams would be realized and it would be so. In high school, I began to see, for the very first time, that the world was not so fair and just as I had always assumed. I found myself experiencing feelings of powerlessness and vulnerability. As a female, in particular, I felt boxed in by society's expectations and constraints.

Upon escaping from high school I began to replace my pessimism with passion. I started to conduct research and read interesting books that spoke of the hopelessness and hatred pervading our world. For the past 4 years, I have spent a great deal of time educating myself and grappling with difficult issues involving race, class, and gender. Part of my decision to become a teacher was influenced by my desire to introduce children to these issues. It was my hope that while portraying an honest though sometimes grim picture of humanity, I might also replace blind acceptance with a sense of empowerment and a hunger for change.

I knew very early on in the year that I wanted to engage my students in antibias activities and lessons that would build on each other throughout the year. Identifying the question I was seeking to answer, however, proved to be a very long and searching process. Although I'd read multiple theorists that suggested children were capable of engaging in lessons of this nature, I didn't really have any first hand experience. I was comforted by the words of Louis Derman-Sparks (1989), who stated: "We know enough not to underestimate the power of children to perceive the negative messages in their world or the power of those messages to harm them" (p. 10).

Initially, I had many questions: Are third graders capable of discussing difficult and controversial issues? How do I begin to engage them in this process? Which activities lend themselves to such an exploration? I answered several of these questions in the first few months of my inquiry and my original queries were replaced by more complex questions. I wanted to know the role of developmentally appropriate practice in implementing an antibias curriculum approach as well as the role of the district curriculum in determining the events and issues I could introduce. It was only in analyzing and reflecting on the data I'd collected that I realized the wondering I was pursuing. What began as a project primarily geared toward the thoughts and ideas of children became an inquiry into my own evolution as a teacher of antibias curriculum. (Hosfeld, 2000)

Andrea's commitment to issues of social justice emerged out of her own political stance and ideology demonstrating the intersection between the role of teacher beliefs and inquiry into issues of social justice.

Andrea's work presents another important lesson about finding and developing your first wondering. She notes that her questions changed and emerged over time. This is a very common occurrence in teacher research. Therefore, understand that as you work diligently to find, develop, and conduct your first inquiry question, your question(s) may change and emerge. This is a totally natural part of the inquiry process. Consequently, as you proceed with your inquiry, you may find that the question you originally develop no longer suits your work or captures the most powerful components of what you are learning. Remember, you may still be "finding" your question. Be prepared to recognize and embrace an emerging question by remaining calm and flexible. You can return to your original questions and modify or change them throughout the duration of your inquiry.

Passion 7 Exercises

1. Look closely at the demographics of the students you teach. Pick a subset of them (e.g., gender, race, class, or disability) and pay particular attention to them during the day. Record in a journal your general observations and emerging questions. Do these children all experience schooling in a similar way?

2. Brainstorm a list of units/topic you teach. Investigate the content of the resources you are using to teach these units. What perspectives seem to be present or missing (e.g., gender, race, class, and disability)? Then analyze each unit by asking yourself how these resources and activities support diversity, democracy, and literacy opportunities for all students.

3. Write down your philosophy of how you prepare your students to become democratic citizens. What role does teaching children about democracy play in your classroom? To what extent does your classroom encourage the development of participation and character traits central to a democratic citizen?

Passion 8: Focus on Understanding the Teaching and Learning Context

An important feature of teacher inquiry is that inquiry occurs within a context and that a context represents a particular classroom within a particular school, within a particular state, and within a particular country. Some teachers' "felt difficulties" actually emerge as a result of these contextual characteristics that influence their teaching. For example, a highly diverse classroom or school may lead a teacher to inquire into understanding the diverse cultures within the classroom and school community in order to better provide instruction, communication, or relationship development. Two prospective teachers, who were interning in a low socioeconomic status school, investigated the feelings of various stakeholders around ebonics in their classroom and school:

We were nervous about the topic of ebonics. As two white novice teachers we were not sure how to respond to the speech of some of our students. We wanted to be sensitive and affirming of their identity but we also struggled with how to prepare them for citizenship responsibilities. As a result, we decided to explore the question of, "How can we respond to student use of ebonics in an appropriate and sensitive way that allows them to gain the participative skills necessary for citizenship?" . . . We explored this question by interviewing many different school and community members—parents, counselors, veteran teachers, administrators . . . we also read a lot of literature on the subject. What we developed was a continuum of responses that we believe both honor and extend our work with these students. (Fieldnotes, PK)

Another example of how context can be the source of an inquiry question emerges as teachers respond to state and national accountability pressures. For example, many teachers in states where pressure from high-stakes testing seems to dominate the culture of the district and schools wonder, "How can we make learning relevant and motivating in a context where testing seems to dominate curriculum and scheduling?" Another question, emerging within the same context, included, "How can I maintain an inclusive classroom when high-stakes testing seems to encourage noninclusive practices?" As teachers recognize the role of context and its impact on their teaching, teachers can use inquiry to identify ways to accommodate, merge, or deflect contextual influences that influence their work in the classroom. Teacher inquiry provides context sensitive tools to do just this.

Passion 8 Exercises

1. Make a three-column list.

Challenge Within Your Context	Felt Difficulty	Wondering

After brainstorming a list of contextual challenges, identify the frustrations that you can potentially influence at either a student, classroom, or school level.

As indicated, these eight passions are not discrete entities, and as noted, many of these inquiries cross borders into multiple passions. We offer these eight passions as lenses for you to use in looking at your own teaching. As you use the passions as lenses, think about each passion as a pair of glasses that you try on as you look at your teaching. For example, if you try on the "social justice glasses," you will search for classroom wonderings around issues of race, class, gender, or disability. If you try on the "curriculum glasses," you will develop a curriculum-related question. Developing an inquiry stance toward teaching relies on teachers becoming active in problematizing each of the lenses or passions. These multiple lenses provide prospective and practicing teachers with a framework for systematically examining their daily work.

WHAT HAPPENS IF I STILL CANNOT LOCATE MY WONDERING?

If you are struggling to find your question independently, the next step is to collaborate and talk to other educators. Although the exercises and descriptions of the passions provide lenses into different aspects of teaching and learning, independently exploring each of the lenses without engaging in discussion with others may still not lead to a question. The exploration of these passions can become more provocative if you collaboratively discuss them with others. For example, if you are a veteran teacher, you might discuss the passions with your team mates, resource teachers, administrators, or university partners. If you are a prospective teacher, you might talk with other prospective teachers, your mentor, field advisor, or other university teacher educators. In the excerpt below, Lisa Malaggese's mentor-teacher, Christina Clair, offers a first inquiry question that starts Lisa's inquiry journey:

> "What are you planning to do for your inquiry project?" As my mentor, Christina, asked me this question, my mind was pretty blank. It was something I had thought about numerous times before, but I had not found anything that had jumped out at me. When the inquiry project had been initially described to us, it sounded as though the topic for my inquiry would be as obvious as a blinking neon sign. For some people, I am sure that this is how they come upon the topics for their inquiries. I saw no such blinking sign. When I searched my brain, looking for possible wonderings, nothing really stood out as something that I desperately wanted to find the answers to.
>
> So, when Christina asked me this question, I told her I honestly did not know. She mentioned that something she had always been interested in was taking a more in-depth approach to teaching

first graders fractions. At first, I said that could be interesting, but that I was not sure what I wanted to do yet. Christina made it clear that it was my decision and that she would help me with whatever I decided to do. I was still waiting for my neon sign. As our classes devoted to inquiry started, with my neon sign nowhere in sight, I started thinking more about Christina's fraction idea.

"Teaching fractions to first graders could be interesting," I thought. The mathematics education course I had taken had left me with a lot of unanswered questions about how to teach mathematics. Even though there is a big focus in my mentor's classroom on the children's understanding of mathematical concepts, I still did not feel confident with my ability to teach math. I decided that the questions I had and my lack of confidence could best be addressed through the actual teaching and designing of math lessons. I hoped that the information I learned about teaching mathematics would also hold true for other subject areas. That way, I could improve my teaching, and thereby my confidence in teaching in all subject areas.

After much consideration, I decided to go ahead with exploring fractions. All right, I had a topic. Now what? What was it *really* that I was trying to find out? After brainstorming with Christina, we came up with our overall question: "Can fractions be taught conceptually to primary students?" I was very proud of that question until it was pointed out to me that it could be a question that could be easily answered with a simple "yes" or "no." I reworked the question; and my official wonderings became "How does one teach fractions conceptually, and what are the impacts of that teaching on the different learners in my classroom?"

At that point, I would not say I was exactly jumping with excitement about my topic. However, I knew it was something that would prove to be interesting and challenging. I think some of my initial lack of excitement stemmed from my disappointment that my neon sign had never come. Little did I know that it really was there; I just had not turned on the switch yet! (Malaggese, 2001)

Lisa's excerpt presents two final important lessons about the development of your initial wondering. First, note how Lisa reframed her first wondering from a dichotomous yes/no question (e.g., "Can fractions be taught conceptually to primary students?") to an open-ended "How do I?" and accompanying companion question (e.g., "How do I teach fractions conceptually, and what are the impacts of that teaching on the different learners in my classroom?"). Rarely does any teacher researcher eloquently state his or her wondering immediately. It takes time, brainstorming, and actually "playing" with your question. Based on our work with teacher-inquirers and the work of Hubbard and Power (1999, p. 28), we suggest the following core principles for finding and refining a teacher research question:

- Look at your teaching through each of the eight lenses.

- Realize that your question might change over the course of your inquiry.

- Ask only real questions. Do not do research to confirm teaching practice you already believe is good or bad. Ask questions whose answers you do not know.

- Develop open-ended rather than yes/no questions.

- Eliminate jargon.

- Be careful to ask a question that your methods can actually explore.

- Avoid value-laden words, or talk your questions over with others since talking helps to clarify the question.

- Be patient with careful articulation of your wondering(s). By playing with the wording of your question, you often fine-tune and discover more detail about the subject you are really passionate about understanding. It is often helpful to engage in a dialogue with a critical friend (a teaching colleague, mentor-teacher, student teacher, or university supervisor). Once you have a wondering committed to paper, ask your critical friend to question you about your inquiry topic. The dialogue that transpires will help you refine your thinking.

Finally, notice in Lisa's work that sometimes a passion for your work will not independently develop from the outset of your inquiry journey. Yet, based on our years of experience helping prospective teachers and practicing teachers engage in inquiry for the first time, we are confident that, as in Lisa's case above, a passion for your work will develop. So, as you end this chapter, take heart from the fact that you have completed one of the most difficult parts of your journey—identifying an inquiry question. Now that you have started your travels, in the next chapter we mark possible routes for conducting your inquiry by summarizing forms that inquiry may take as well as noting forms of collaboration you can establish to support your inquiry journey. These summaries may help you further refine your wondering(s) and chart the remainder of your inquiry travels.

To Collaborate or   3
Not to Collaborate:
That Is the
Question!

Whether or not you are a Shakespeare fan, you are likely familiar with the famous soliloquy spoken by Hamlet that begins, "To be or not to be, that is the question." As teacher-inquirers begin formulating their initial wonderings, they often ponder in a similar fashion: "To collaborate or not to collaborate, that is the next teacher inquiry question."

As is the case in much of Shakespeare's work, when characters such as Hamlet begin a soliloquy, they pose a rhetorical question. A rhetorical question is asked for effect and neither expects nor requires an answer. Shakespeare would often evoke this literary device to allow his characters to use language effectively and persuasively, resulting in the audience's "eavesdropping" on the character's thinking and gaining insight into character traits that are vital to the development of the story.

In the style of Shakespeare, we have used the rhetorical question, "To collaborate or not to collaborate?" in the titling of this chapter, because it is a question you need not answer. No teacher-inquirer should spend time pondering whether he or she should collaborate, because when engaging in teacher inquiry, the answer to this question is always an unequivocal yes! Rather, we pose this question to help you consider how you will collaborate. As you complete this chapter, we hope, like Shakespeare's audiences' gaining insight into his key character, you will gain insights into how collaboration supports and enhances your teacher inquiry.

WHY IS COLLABORATION SO IMPORTANT?

> If you investigate the work of any teacher-researcher who has
> sustained his or her work over time, you quickly see another
> person, or many other people, standing in the shadows. Virtually
> all teacher-researchers depend on a partner or a group who
> shares their passions and provides reassurance when a project
> bogs down. (Hubbard & Power, 1999)

Similarly, in our work with teacher-inquirers, we have identified at
least four good reasons why when you look at any single teacher-inquirer,
he or she is standing in the company of others. Consider these four reasons
why you should seek out support as you continue on your inquiry journey.

Reason 1: Research Is Hard Work!

With the resurgence of interest since the early 1990s in teacher
research (Cochran-Smith & Lytle, 1999), and its popularity as a professional growth tool for the initial preparation and continuing education of
teachers, getting caught up in the teacher research movement is easy. As
you know, the work of a teacher is quite demanding! To date, teacher
inquiry has not traditionally been a part of teachers' practice. Hence,
engaging in inquiry potentially adds an additional layer into the already-
crowded work life of a teacher: "Participation in teacher research requires
considerable effort by innovative and dedicated teachers to stay in their
classrooms and at the same time carve out opportunities to inquire and
reflect on their practice" (Cochran-Smith & Lytle, 1993). This inquiry
work becomes a quiet form of teacher leadership that contributes to
disrupting the status quo and inciting change.

While we believe it is critical to make teacher inquiry *a part of* your
teaching rather than *apart from* your teaching, the fact remains that even if
you are able to seamlessly integrate teaching and inquiry (as we believe
should be the case!), the work is difficult and can be quite draining at times.
Through collaboration with others, teacher-inquirers find a crucial source
of energy and support that keeps them going and sustains their work.

Reason 2: Teacher Talk Is Important!

Teachers talk all the time! They talk with their students by posing
questions, delivering information, giving directions, and facilitating
discussions each day. They talk with their colleagues, "swapping classroom stories, sharing specific ideas, seeking one another's advice, and

trading opinions about issues and problems in their own schools and the larger educational arena" (Cochran-Smith & Lytle, 1993, p. 94). They talk with administrators to solve problems and identify support that is necessary for success in the classroom. They talk with parents about expectations, their child's progress, and ways to work together to facilitate a child's growth. Talk consumes almost every moment of a teacher's day.

Similarly, the talk of teacher inquiry also becomes "a part of" each teacher's day. In Chapter 2 you learned the importance of talking with another person as you defined and refined your first questions and the focus of your inquiry. Similarly, as you continue on in the teacher research journey, engaging in dialog with another professional will heighten your awareness of knowledge you've generated about teaching that you now take for granted, making what you know more visible to yourself and to others. Making your tacit knowledge more visible can often lead to significant discoveries when you are individually or collaboratively analyzing and interpreting your data.

In addition, talking with another professional may help you call into question assumptions or "givens" about teaching practice, a process that is critical to making your teaching problematic through the process of inquiry. According to Cochran-Smith and Lytle (1993), "the givens of schooling compose a long list, including reading groups, rostering, inservicing, tracking, abilities, disabilities, mastery, retention, promotion, giftedness, disadvantage, special needs, departmentalization, 47-minute periods, coverage, standards, detention, teacher-proof materials, and homework" (p. 96). Teacher talk enables teachers to examine and critique these "givens" in education. In talking with others, you are able to generate possible alternatives to practice as well as consider different interpretations that help every teacher gain perspective as his or her inquiry unfolds.

Reason 3: There's Safety in Numbers!

Knowledge is power. Through teacher inquiry, you are taking charge of your own professional growth and generating knowledge that can be supported with evidence. While this is one of the most exciting components of teacher inquiry, it can also become extremely stressful, as it is quite probable that the new knowledge you construct from your study may threaten the status quo and become threatening to other's assumptions about professional practice.

For example, perhaps you complete a curriculum piece that generates new practices that many of your colleagues are anxious to incorporate, but the principal who selected and designed the original unit for your district feels that his or her personal authority and position as an educator are threatened by your findings. You face a litany of obstacles thrown out by your administrator and a long list of reasons why you can't teach the unit in the way that your evidence shows is most effective. If an inquiry leads to controversy, collaboration with other teachers can provide you personal and professional support as you share your findings and combat others who are resistant to change: Remember, change requires a critical mass.

Reason 4: There's Strength in Numbers!

Just as there is safety in numbers, there is also strength in numbers. While it *is* possible for one person's inquiry to lead to large-scale and schoolwide change, it is often not probable when resistance to change is present (as noted in the example presented in the previous paragraph). However, when communities of teacher-inquirers begin to build on each other's work, findings become more difficult to ignore or resist:

> Communities of teacher researchers can play an essential role in school reform. Not only does their work add to the knowledge base on teaching, but their collective power as knowledge-generating communities also influences broader school policies regarding curriculum, assessment, school organization, and home-school linkages. Through teacher-research communities, teachers' voices play a more prominent part in the dialogue of school reform. (Cochran-Smith & Lytle, 1993, p. 103)

Hence, any inquiry you engage in becomes stronger when connected to a collection of related inquiries generated by other teacher-researchers. This strength is made possible through your collaboration with others.

In addition, sometimes, when inquiries do not go as planned, you garner strength by continuing to work with colleagues. For example, Larry Rotz, Mary Robert, Judi Kur, and Marcia Heitzmann collaborated on an inquiry that focused on effectively integrating SMART Board technology into their curriculum. When confronted with the tremendous time necessary to troubleshoot and problem-solve the SMART Board technology, they made little progress on the initial wondering: "How can we effectively integrate SMART Board technology into our curriculum?" Working in isolation, they might have easily "called it quits" when faced with so many technical difficulties. Together, though, they found the strength to forge ahead and changed their initial wondering from focusing on the integration of the SMART Board into the curriculum to focusing on how collaboration can be used to provide support for teachers interested in taking risks and experimenting with the SMART Board. At the close of their project, they reflected as follows:

> How many teachers does it take to plug in a SMART Board? With all of the technology difficulties we experienced at the start of our project, the answer to this question was all four of us! Through the process of collaborating in this inquiry, however, we were able to schedule time to work together, become risk takers, and experiment with new technology. Because of this positive experience, we will look for ways to continue to collaborate not only with technology and inquiry, but in other areas of curriculum. We plan to continue to use the SMART Board to increase our comfort level and confidence in using this technology. As we gain more confidence and experience, we are excited to begin sharing what we have learned with other teachers in our building. We are all ready, willing and eager to help other teachers use this new technology in their classrooms. We have even returned to our original wondering and have begun to enhance our curriculum by developing lessons using the SMART Board . . . . We are excited about being on the cutting edge of this new technology and the possibilities it holds for improving instruction. We are just as excited about the opportunities to continue our collaboration. It still may take four teachers to plug in a SMART Board, but only because we realize the benefits of working together. (Rotz, Kur, Robert, & Heitzmann, 2002)

These four teachers' collaboration and reframing of their question enabled their continued exploration of classroom uses of SMART Board technology.

WHAT ARE THE POSSIBILITIES
FOR HOW I MIGHT COLLABORATE?

Schools are often structured in ways that promote teacher isolation rather than collaboration (Lortie, 1975). Teachers spend the majority of their day working within the four walls of their classrooms. Yet, every teacher's classroom is located within a building that contains many other classrooms. Consequently, as they work within the four walls of their rooms, right beside them or across the hall are other teachers who engage in the same work each day. Hence, the work of teachers is literally a "side-by-side" endeavor, offering many potential colleagues who can join with one another to inquire into practice.

In addition to the side-by-side work of teachers within the same school building, side-by-side work may occur in a single classroom. For example, spurred by the inclusion movement, many general education classroom teachers are now coteaching with special education teachers to provide appropriate instruction for all students within an entire class. Similarly, as efforts are made to reduce class size, teachers are often paired with full-time paraprofessionals to provide more individual attention to each student. Another example of side-by-side work of teachers occurs when schools and universities partner in the preparation of new teachers by integrating student-teachers or interns into the room to complete field work. The side-by-side nature of the work of both veteran and beginning teachers within one school building or within one classroom can provide natural opportunities for collaboration in the systematic study of their own teaching practice. The following four logical structures, for veterans and/or beginning teachers to partner in inquiry, can provide the support necessary for encouraging inquiry (Dana, 2001).

Collaborative Structure 1: Shared Inquiry

Having interest(s) in common with another professional lays the foundation for the first configuration for collaboration—*shared inquiry*. Shared inquiry occurs when two practicing teachers, two prospective teachers, or a prospective and a practicing teacher pair define and conduct a single teacher research project together.

An imperative component of any teacher inquiry is that it must evoke passion from the teacher-inquirer. Thus, a prerequisite for engaging in shared inquiry is a shared passion across two or more individuals for the same topic. One example of shared inquiry is the work of Amy Jones and Diane Reed, previously introduced in Chapter 2. Recall that Amy and Diane shared a passion for finding ways to teach about Columbus in a developmentally appropriate way. As two fourth-grade teachers within the same building, they discovered during an after-school grade-level meeting that they both shared "felt difficulties" about the upcoming unit on explorers. Diane noted that she was disturbed that the encounter between Columbus and the Taino people was not developed in the unit. Amy echoed this concern and also noted that she was unsure which components of the unit to emphasize, given the constraint that the unit needed to fit within a four-week time period. Each teacher was committed to resolving her dilemma. Their shared dilemma and passion for this topic led to their collaborative completion of an inquiry in this area (Jones & Reed, 2000).

Amy and Diane's collaboration exemplifies two practicing teachers working together. An example of shared inquiry by a prospective and a practicing teacher pair is found in the work of Sheila Abruzzo, a 12-year veteran and mentor-teacher in a professional development school, and her intern, Missy Koziak (Koziak & Abruzzo, 2000). As Missy interned with Sheila in her first-grade classroom during the 1999-2000 school year, both were intrigued by technology and the possibilities technology might hold for enhancing parent communication. Together, they explored, compared, and contrasted newsletters, home/school journals, and Web sites, as well as other strategies that enhance the teaching partnership between home and school. Each teacher had different areas of strength to contribute to their shared inquiry. Missy had learned a great deal about creating Web sites as part of her PDS methods coursework in the fall, and Sheila, with 12 years of teaching experience, had extensive experience in talking with and providing written materials for parents. Through their inquiry, they created a symbiotic relationship where they met, discussed, created, pondered, and analyzed different modes and varieties of parent communication that neither intern nor mentor could undertake on her own. Sheila shares that the most outstanding component of engaging in shared inquiry was the ability to lead and learn from each other.

In a similar fashion, mentor-teacher Darice Hampton and her intern Beth Schickel decided to conduct a joint inquiry project when Darice was enrolled in a graduate teacher inquiry course at the university and Beth was completing a teacher inquiry requirement for student teaching at the same time. They recall the process that led them to engage in shared inquiry as well as the benefits they reaped from conducting a single teacher inquiry project together as follows:

> As a mentor and intern, we observe our students daily and sub-consciously are participating in informal inquiry all the time. Each day, we discuss happenings in the classroom, not only to bounce ideas off of each other but also to gain a different perspective. When we decided to begin formal inquiry, we naturally began bouncing ideas off one another. When our wonderings seemed to mesh, we decided to complete our inquiry project together.

> When we began to map out our journey, the first step of developing phonemic awareness activities for two children in our class was one benefit from our collaboration. By working together, we doubled the number of creative ideas for activity development. From this step forward, our daily discussion led us to alter our activities based on student response, as well as discover our

learnings and follow our new wonderings. Without the collaboration involved in the project, our phonemic awareness work with two students may have taken a different, less informed direction, as it was through our discussions that we were able to process our field notes in a way that allowed us to see different perspectives and interpretations of what was occurring. Many times, the sharing of our differing perspectives led each of us to new insights and subsequent changes in the phonemic strategies we were using with the children that we would not have discovered had we been working alone. It has been the partnership we have created through the PDS that has allowed for our wondering to be addressed and our learnings to be publicly shared. Being coauthors of this inquiry has given us the opportunity to become teacher researchers and to take our wonderings to a new level through our teamwork. (Hampton & Schickel, 2002)

A final example of shared inquiry indicates the ways two *prospective* teachers might work together. After being classmates in a science methods course in the fall semester, Rebecca Roberts and Lindsay Elliot discovered that the commitment they had made to teach science through inquiry in that course was easier said then done when they began their student teaching semester. Rebecca and Lindsay's shared experience in the science methods course and subsequent desire to implement what they had learned about teaching science as inquiry led them to complete one joint inquiry project. Working together, their goal was to analyze their questioning, reflect on their students' responses, and decide whether the questions they posed were promoting science as inquiry:

With a full dose of SCIED 458 under our belt, we were walking away from our methods classes last December all pumped up and ready to teach science through inquiry. What we didn't realize, however, was the fact that we couldn't reach the top of that mountain without first grabbing on to some stepping-stones to make our way up. We understood the perks of teaching science through inquiry but we didn't understand that every single topic within science would not necessarily lend itself to inquiry. We didn't realize that we couldn't just jump into science and expect to change our methods of teaching by throwing in a few experiments and—*poof*—inquiry would magically appear.

After watching previous videos of our teaching from our science ed course and comparing them to the lessons we recently taught during our student teaching semester, it became clear that some areas of science are just more difficult to teach through inquiry than others. This became particularly evident as we watched our sink-and-float lessons completed in October. It was simple. We were not even aware of our questioning and we were automatically asking questions such as, "How could we turn this sinker into a floater?" and "What made the boat that held more marbles a better floater than others?" It was plain to see that these questions really did ignite the students' thinking and probe them to further consider each of the factors going into the creation of their clay boats.

On the other hand, while both being fully aware of the questions we were to be asking during the first couple of lessons of our *Wonderful World of Nature* unit in March, we were stumbling upon questions such as, what is a beak? Do we have them? Do you think birds have better vision than us? And do all birds fly? Fortunately we can laugh with each other about these questions now, but at the time, even though we knew that every word out of our mouth was leading to a very unproductive question, it was not clear to us as to how we should go about turning them into productive ones. As mentioned before, after a lot of experimenting with different kinds of questions and analyzing the effectiveness of each of the types we were asking, we were successful in turning this unit into an inquiry-based one despite the fact that it was initially a very difficult task for us to accomplish. (Roberts & Elliot, 2002, pp. 13-14).

Through collaborating on one joint inquiry project, Lindsay and Rebecca provided support for each other as they discovered inherent difficulties of teaching science as inquiry. In addition, they provided "comic relief" for each other ("Fortunately, we can laugh with each other about these questions now . . .") as they viewed their videos during data analysis. One benefit of shared inquiry is being able to find humor in your work with a colleague, especially when your inquiry leads to some unsettling realizations about your teaching.

Collaborative Structure 2: Parallel Inquiry

A shared passion for a single topic between two or more prospective and practicing teachers does not always emerge since all teachers are unique individuals who share different interests and passions. In addition, collaboration between prospective and practicing teachers such as those noted earlier are not often practical as veterans and novices are at very different places developmentally, and this may naturally lead to completely different passions for teacher inquiry. If teachers in the same building or classroom hold different passions, then they may choose to engage in *parallel inquiry*.

Parallel inquiry occurs when teacher pairs (prospective teacher pairs, practicing teacher pairs, or a prospective and a practicing teacher pair) conduct two parallel but individual teacher research projects, working collectively to support each other's individual endeavors. Parallel inquiry comes from the "parallel play" concept discussed in the early childhood literature. In parallel play, two toddlers may sit in a sandbox, just inches apart from each other, and be enthralled with their individual exploration of the sand. They are each individually immersed in their own activity within the same physical space. Likewise, when you engage in parallel inquiry, your playmate is a fellow teacher, your sand is the complexities inherent in teaching, and your sandbox is the same school or classroom. Unlike parallel play, however, where the two toddlers are often oblivious of each other and rarely interact as they play, when engaging in parallel inquiry, teachers support each other's individual endeavors by engaging in such activities as collecting data for each other, discussing data analysis and findings, and teaching for each other to provide the time necessary for each individual to engage in his or her own individual inquiry.

For example, recall from Chapter 2 that Judi Kur was passionate about making her delivery of a prehistoric life-forms unit more inquiry oriented. At the time of this inquiry, Judi was working with an intern, Corinne Almquist. Although supportive of and interested in Judi's work, Corrine was not passionate about participating in the curriculum revision of that particular unit. As a result, Judi's intern completed a separate inquiry project that she was passionate about (Almquist, 2000). Although their inquiries were separate, both intern and mentor supported each other's work by collecting data for each other, discussing data analysis and findings, and teaching for each other to provide the time necessary for each individual to engage in her inquiries.

Similarly, recall intern Andrea Hosfeld's passion for teaching social justice and her quest to gain insights into implementing an antibias curriculum through her inquiry project presented in Chapter 2. Andrea's mentor-teacher, Kimber Mitchell, was also interested in defining and conducting a teacher inquiry project at the time of Andrea's inquiry and was an accomplished teacher of social studies with expertise and interest in Andrea's topic. A logical deduction might be that Kimber and

Andrea would engage in shared inquiry, collaborating on a single inquiry project. Yet, realizing that teaching social studies was already one of her areas of strength, Kimber supported her intern but focused her own inquiry energies on further developing another area of her teaching—the effective teaching of science through a unit on air and aviation (Mitchell, 2000). While individually inquiring into different subject areas simultaneously, Kimber and Andrea supported and learned from each other in much the same ways as Judi and Corinne. In this classroom, parallel inquiry also became a mechanism for exploring the teaching of two different subject matters. Imagine the benefit to the children in this classroom that year as science and social studies teaching were being investigated simultaneously through inquiry!

Collaborative Structure 3: Intersecting Inquiry

In parallel inquiry, two or more teachers are engaging in inquiry on completely different topics. Sometimes teachers engage in individual inquiry projects that focus on the same topic, but explore different questions and wonderings about that topic. When this happens, a potential exists for inquiries to intersect and collaboration to occur at the juncture of that intersection.

We return to teacher-inquirer Judi Kur to illustrate intersecting inquiries. The year after she completed her inquiry on teaching dinosaurs, Judi and long-time first-grade teaching partner and friend Marsha Heitzmann were both interested in using peer coaching to help them gain insights into their teaching of reading. They decided to engage in a shared teacher inquiry project to develop and explore their peer coaching relationship and the ways this relationship could contribute to their own understandings of who they were as teachers of reading.

At this time, they made an appointment to meet with their principal, Deirdre Bauer, to share with her their upcoming plans for inquiry. Deirdre met their inquiry idea with enthusiasm and support and shared that she had been interested in the notion of peer coaching for years as well. Furthermore, intrigued by witnessing the ways teacher inquiry can lead to powerful learning, Deirdre wished to conduct her own teacher inquiry project this year. Ironically, she wanted to explore the role principals can play in facilitating professional development through peer coaching. What transpired was the development of two separate inquiries that crossed one another. Judi and Marsha focused on developing a peer coaching relationship and using that relationship to gain insights into the ways reading instruction played out in their classroom. Deirdre focused on studying the peer coaching relationship as it developed in two of her

Developing a
Research Plan:
Making Inquiry a
Part of Your
Teaching Practice

4

O nce a teacher-inquirer has selected a focus for his or her work, defined a wondering to pursue, and located himself or herself within one of the inquiry support structures, the next step in the journey is learning about data collection and developing a plan for the study. Meaningful teacher inquiry should not "depart from" the daily work of classroom teachers, but become "a part of" their daily work. Hence, selecting the data collection strategies you will use for your study simply means thinking about life in the classroom/school and the ways life in the classroom/school can be naturally "captured" as data.

WHAT DO DATA LOOK LIKE,
HOW DO I COLLECT THEM, AND HOW
DO THEY FIT INTO MY WORK AS A TEACHER?

In this section, we share seven common strategies teacher-researchers use for capturing "the data of" life in schools. Each strategy is demonstrated through the work of one or more teacher-inquirers. Some examples come from teachers you have already met in previous chapters, while others introduce new teachers and their inquiry projects as examples for illustrating particular types of data collection. Once again, as we share excerpts from these teachers' work, we point to lessons learned about data collection so as to offer you practical suggestions and guidance about this component of the inquiry process.

Strategy 1: Fieldnotes

In the previous chapter, we noted that the life of a classroom teacher is quite demanding when we discussed the first reason for collaboration—teaching and engaging in inquiry is hard work! One of the reasons the work of teaching is so demanding is that schools and classrooms are busy places, jam-packed with "action." Teachers inter*act* with children, children inter*act* with each other, and teachers and children inter*act* with subject matter, and all of these inter*actions* occur within a particular context that is mediated by values (e.g., all children can learn), norms (e.g., students must raise their hands and be called on before answering a question), and rituals (e.g., each morning, the class salutes the flag).

To capture "action" in the classroom, many teacher-researchers take fieldnotes as they observe. Fieldnotes can come in many shapes, forms, and varieties. Some of these include scripting dialog and conversation, diagramming the classroom or a particular part of the classroom, noting what a child or children are doing at particular time intervals (e.g., every 2 minutes), and recording every question that a teacher asks. Fieldnotes are not interpretations but rather focus on capturing what is occurring without commenting as to why the action might be occurring or how one judges a particular act.

The form(s) that your fieldnotes take depend on your wondering. For instance, in Nancy Sunner's study of her questioning techniques, her fieldnotes listed every question she asked during selected lessons. The connections between your wondering and the form your fieldnotes take will become more apparent in subsequent examples of fieldnotes shared throughout this section.

You may take fieldnotes as you engage in the teaching act or have them taken for you by others. An example of fieldnotes taken by teachers as they inquired comes from the work of intern Beth Schickel and mentor Darice Hampton introduced in the previous chapter. Recall that Beth and Darice were interested in the development of phonemic awareness in two of their kindergarten learners. As they worked with these children, one way they took fieldnotes was by scripting the responses the children had to different phonemic awareness activities. One activity they developed for these learners involved finding pictures with the same initial phonemes. To illustrate scripting a child's response, an excerpt from their scripted fieldnotes that was collected during this activity is shared in Figure 4.1.

Figure 4.1   Scripted Fieldnotes by Darice and Beth

Scripting as a form of fieldnotes simply involves writing down verbatim (or as close to verbatim as possible) what your learners are saying. The first time you script notes for yourself, it may feel awkward or unnatural. Some of the teacher-inquirers we know have found little "tricks" to help in the process. For example, when Amy Ruth was scripting at the kindergarten writing table, she found the children were more interested in what and why she was writing than in completing their own work. Frustrated after her first attempt to collect data by scripting, as it seemed to interfere more with her teaching than help her inquire into her teaching, she found a way to fold data collection unobtrusively into her teaching in the following way. Amy constructed a red folder that looked just like the red folders all of her kindergarteners worked in at their writing center. The cover of the red folder Amy constructed for herself was marked in big black magic marker letters as follows: "Miss Ruth's Writing Folder." She shared the folder with her students, noting that over the next few weeks, "Miss Ruth is going to be writing at the writing center just like you! When you do your writing, I will be doing mine." Amy used that folder when engaged in scripting, and the children understood that Miss Ruth was working just like they were and never questioned her about it again.

Similarly, another kindergarten teacher-inquirer we know, Lynn Dobash, became frustrated when she discovered that important actions she wanted to capture never occurred in a single sitting, but rather were sprinkled throughout her day. It was not practical for Lynn to run to her desk to grab her field notebook each time she wanted to make a note. To solve this problem, she began wearing a very fashionable necklace—a yellow Post-it note pad with a pen attached. When a child said or did something that she wished to capture, she simply jotted it down on a post-it note and continued on in her teaching. At the end of the day, she stuck each Post-it in her notebook. A little ingenuity can go a long way when making data collection a part of, not apart from, your teaching.

Sometimes, unlike Amy and Lynn, some teacher-inquirers just cannot find a comfortable way to take fieldnotes for themselves, or they want to capture action when they are an integral part of that action (e.g., giving directions, leading a discussion, asking questions, etc.). In these cases, it is impossible to record in writing your own directions as you are giving them or your own questions as you pose them. If this is the case for you, two other options are available: (1) video- or audiotape yourself or (2) find a colleague to help script the observation for you. If you are recording, you will tape, watch the tape later, and transcribe what has occurred by taking notes or enlisting another person to script notes from the tape for you. While watching or listening to yourself on video- or audiotape can be extremely insightful, many teacher-inquirers we know find it difficult to make this a part of their teaching and opt for having others take notes for them instead. For example, intern Gail Romig and mentor-teacher Brian Peters were engaged in a shared inquiry project to investigate the ways they might use science talks to enhance student understanding of science concepts. Early in their inquiry, they audiotaped the science talks as they occurred, but changed to taking turns scripting the talks for each other as follows:

> Throughout our inquiry process, we took turns facilitating the talks and gathering data. While one person sat with the group and helped to guide the conversation, the other person sat outside the circle and kept track of who was talking and what kind of information they were sharing. The person who collected data sat outside the circle so as to not distract or intimidate the students. If the students thought their ideas were being judged or scrutinized, perhaps they would not have been as likely to share. This seemed to be the reaction of some children when they knew they were being tape-recorded.

> Early on we tape-recorded a few of our Science Talks. It seemed, however, that some students were reluctant to talk when they saw the microphone. During one of our small group talks later in the marking period, one child asked why we don't tape record the talks anymore. Gail told him that it seemed like people were afraid

to talk if they thought they were being recorded. The student said that he didn't like to talk when we recorded because he thought his voice "sounded dumb" on tape.

In addition to students being uncomfortable with tape recording, we found that listening to the tapes in the evening after school was insightful but too time consuming and not worth the time it was taking to rehash the entirety of the Science Talk discussion. Audio taping captured more than we needed to capture. To gain insights into our wondering, we just needed to know who was talking and what type of talk it seemed to be. Consequently, we developed a system for taking fieldnotes that involved noting who was talking, paraphrasing what was said, and coding the comment with one of three different codes: "S" for simple, "D" for detailed, "R" for repeat, and "0" for no response. Along with this system we also made notes of what we observed happening during the talks, for example, if students were sharing with a child next to them. (Peters & Romig, 2001)

Like Amy and Lynn, it took some time for Gail and Brian to find a way to capture the action in their classroom in their fieldnotes that was comfortable for them. For two sound reasons (i.e., some students feeling self-conscious and the time-consuming nature of listening to the tapes), they moved from audiotaping as a form of data collection to taking fieldnotes for each other. If you choose fieldnotes as one of your data collection strategies, realize that it might take some time and experimentation to find a form of note taking that works for you and for your inquiry.

If you are completing your first inquiry as a prospective teacher currently in student teaching or another field experience practicum, a logical note taker for you may be your university supervisor or cooperating teacher. Over time, traditional visits by your university supervisor can move from the supervisor taking charge of the direction of the observation and providing evaluative feedback to you, to you taking charge of the direction of the observations by sharing with your supervisor the nature of your inquiry question and asking him or her to script certain lessons for you (Silva & Dana, 2001). For example, one way Julie Russell collected data for her study of teaching writing to second graders was by asking her supervisor to make data collection around her inquiry a priority during her weekly observations (see Figure 4.2).

If you do not have another adult readily available in your classroom to take fieldnotes for you and want to collect data in this way, you may need to get a bit more creative. For example, you might adjust your schedule to teach the lesson you would like scripted during the time a fellow teacher

Figure 4.2   Scripted Notes Taken for Julie

PENNSTATE

INQUIRY NOTES:
TARGET 2 areas:
• Rubric
• Brainstorming

COLLEGE *of* EDUCATION

Office of Pre-Service Teaching

p. 1

NAME *Julie Russell*
SUBJECT/GRADE *2*
NO. OF STUDENTS *22*
SCHOOL *MV*

DATE/DAY *3/27/02*
TIME *9:15*
OBSERVER *N Dana*
DISTRICT *SCASD*

What's this check list for?
    To help us write complex stories.

What does a beginning need?
    C - reads
    D - makes your story that people want to read more.
        - characters
    C - dazzling action words
What did endings need?
    E - happy ending
        solve problem
    H - you have a problem that makes sense to your
        story
Are we allowed to use happily ever after?
No - why not?
    K - They need to know more
We're going to read Babbage Rose. Look at your rubric. How
    would you score writer?
Look at this rubric. How did the author do?
    D - can you grab the book and read the first sentence?
A - I'd give it a star
Why?
    Because the sun paints the world
K - What would you give it?
    A work hard on it because it sounds like a research
    book and I don't like research books

friend has a scheduled special or planning period and ask your teacher friend to come in and take notes for you. Fourth-grade teachers Cheryl McCarty and Priya Poehner exemplified this type of creativity and flexibility in their study of peer coaching and the ways engaging in this process could give them insights into questions they held about their teaching. The thought processes Cheryl and Priya each used that led them to a particular form of field noting for each other, as well as an example of that fieldnote form are shared in the following excerpt from their inquiry (McCarty & Poehner, 2002):

Priya's Narrative

My inquiry question focused on one of my lower ability reading groups and their use of the discussion strategies that I had taught them. I was often frustrated that these students were unable to carry on a conversation without me being there to keep them on task and keep the conversation flowing. I was interested in seeing whether this was really the case, and if it was, to get some ideas on how to improve the situation.

I sat down with Cheryl after school one day and talked about the layout and the focus of the observation that she was about to perform. I told her my frustrations with this literature group and mentioned that they were unable to have discussions without books. This was an area of concern as more advanced groups understood and enjoyed the books we were reading at a deeper level as a result of their group discussions. During our discussion, I described and talked about the students in this group so that Cheryl could identify them easily. We talked about where the group usually met, where each of the students sat, my placement within this group, and where I would like her to sit in relation to the group. I mentioned that I was interested in the flow of conversation and was also interested in how much I contributed to the group. My goal was to get the group started by asking a question that I had noted as I read the chapter they had been assigned, and modeling the discussion prompts; and then encouraging them to take turns asking their questions and leading the discussion. I asked Cheryl to use a circular seating chart with arrows to show the direction of the conversation or script of the lesson.

When Cheryl arrived in my classroom, I had already prepared the students so that they would not be unnecessarily distracted by her arrival. She sat in the previously arranged area and was ready to chart the conversation flow. We had decided that she would sit behind me so that she could scan the entire group with ease and observe both body language and verbal participation. [The first page of these notes appear in Figure 4.3.]

Cheryl's Narrative

I chose to inquire into two things: my math teaching and the level of on-task behavior in my classroom . . . . This year I was assigned a challenging math group that has been a constant source of

Figure 4.3   Priya's Fieldnotes

reflection after my teaching day is complete . . . . My math class is a combination of students from three fourth-grade classrooms. The students are a mixture of students who are meeting fourth-grade objectives and are just below fourth-grade benchmarks. The typical student in my math class learns at a slower pace, requires reteaching, and has difficulty with problem solving. It is also important to mention that there are quite a few "strong personalities" in my class and, as a group, are difficult to manage.

Wanting to collect data on a lesson on fractions in my class, I asked Priya to observe me. Since Priya and I work very closely, she was completely aware of the makeup of my math class as well as my teaching style and philosophies for teaching this particular math group. We agreed upon a form for fieldnotes and her location while in my classroom. Noting my concerns that my class was often "off-task" and not attending to my teaching, Priya would take 2-minute sweeps of the room and watch the class as a whole for on-task behavior.

I explained that my math lesson would consist of four different parts: problem solving, fraction concept review, addition of fractions using number lines, and class work and homework. We decided the best way for her to note on-task behavior would be to use a seating chart in which she would mark her observations of each student. [Figure 4.4 shows how she coded her observations in different colors for different parts of the lesson.]

By looking across each fieldnote example that has been shared, we demonstrate that fieldnotes can be as different and varied as the individuals who take them. What is most important is that you select or create a system that works for you in practice and informs your wondering.

Strategy 2: Documents/Artifacts

As indicated, fieldnotes capture actions as data on *paper*. However, even without fieldnotes, schools and classrooms naturally generate a tremendous paper trail that captures much of the daily classroom activity. The paper trail includes student work; curriculum guides; textbooks; teacher manuals; children's literature; IEPs; district memos; parent newsletters; progress reports; teacher plan books; written lesson plans; and correspondence to and from parents, the principal, and specialists. The amount of paperwork that crosses a teacher's desk can make any teacher bleary eyed. Often the papers teachers view do not hold significant meaning when read in isolation or when read quickly in order to be able to hand them back in the morning. Teachers need to "get through" paperwork in order to keep up with their work.

Yet, when teaching and inquiry are intertwined with one another, the papers become data and take on new meaning. When teacher-inquirers

Figure 4.4   Cheryl's Fieldnotes

select and collect the papers that are related to their research wonderings, we call these papers documents or artifacts. Systematically collecting papers provides you with the opportunity to look within and across these documents to analyze them in new and different ways. For example, as a method of tracking student productivity in the classroom, many teachers save student work, stamping dates on the work to know when it was produced.

Through looking at student work over time, claims can be made that could not occur when viewing a single piece of student work in isolation.

Depending on their wondering or the progress of an inquiry, other teacher-researchers might collect student work, noting the context in which it was produced. An illustration of student work as data appears in the teacher inquiry completed by Beth and Darice. As one form of data collection, they saved the papers that the two children who were engaging in phonemic awareness activities produced over time. Two pieces of their data are shown in Figures 4.5 and 4.6.

Through comparing these two artifacts, as well as other data that were produced during their study, Darice and Beth were able to conclude that when Ted was in the company of friends, his illustrations were more detailed and sound spelling was more developed than when Ted didn't strongly socially connect with the children at his table.

As indicated, documents are naturally occurring forms of data that can be extremely powerful. Teacher-inquirers need only decide which naturally produced papers relate to their wonderings and plan a systematic way to collect, label, and organize them.

Strategy 3: Interviews

In Chapter 3, we stated that, "Teacher talk is important!" As talk is crucial to the life of a teacher, capturing talk can be an important form of data collection. Fieldnotes are one way to capture talk that occurs naturally in the classroom. Some teacher-inquirers go one step farther than naturally occurring classroom talk by interviewing as well. Interviewing can be informal and spontaneous or more thoughtfully planned.

When veteran teacher Kimber Mitchell wondered about the effective teaching of science through a unit on air and aviation, she returned to her students at the end of the school year. She used interviews to gain insights into what the students remembered about a particular unit after many months had elapsed as follows:

> During my student interviews I asked my students to tell me about the four forces of flight. Most of them were able to talk about two or three of the forces. None of my students, even the ones who normally have excellent memories, could name all four forces. Their understanding of the forces of flight was sketchier than what they remembered about air. We had only one day of investigations on each of the four forces of flight in contrast to eight lessons related to air. It seems obvious to me that the students need repeated and parallel investigations on the same topic for it to become a part of their

Figure 4.5   Ted—Random Writing Samples From Children at the Writing Center

long-term science knowledge. This means that I have to make choices as a teacher about what things are most important and what things I can leave out. It is a difficult process but one that is helped by returning to one of my original questions: Which investigations help the children to understand how airplanes fly? In an interview, one of my students summed it up this way: "If you do a lot of experiments about one thing and do the experiments over and over (many trials), it will explain things." (Emily Dong in Mitchell, 2000)

Depending on your wondering, interviewing children in the classroom as well as interviewing adults such as parents, administrators, other classroom teachers, and instructional support teachers, can be a rich source of data.

Strategy 4: Focus Groups

Focus groups offer teachers another vehicle for collecting the talk and thoughts of children in the classroom. In many ways, focus groups occur

Figure 4.6   Ted—Writing Samples When Working With Best Friend

daily in the form of whole class or small group discussion. The focus-group discussion can serve as a tool for understanding students' perceptions. For example, a focus group can provide insight into how students experience a new instructional strategy or what prior knowledge students possess about a particular content area. Teachers who use graphic organizers such as "What We Know, What We Want to Know, What We Learned" (K-W-L) strategies are conducting a form of focus group that can serve as a source of data that can inform inquiry. Although focus groups can serve as a quick way to obtain data, focus groups have some limitations. For example, focus groups are more likely to capture breadth of opinion since the goal is often to understand the group's perspective. In addition, sometimes due to the presence of diverging opinions, less confident focus-group members refrain from sharing their thoughts.

Strategy 5: Reflective Journals

Thus far, we have discussed ways to make data collection a part of your teaching by capturing what naturally occurs in your teaching day—action in the classroom through fieldnotes, student progress in your classroom through document analysis, and talk in the classroom or school through interviews and focus groups. One of the ways that interviewing and focus groups serve as powerful data collection strategies is through the *talk* of interviewing, because a teacher-inquirer gains access into the *thinking* of the child or adult being interviewed.

Capturing "thinking" is a challenge for any researcher. One way a teacher-researcher captures the thinking that occurs in the school and classroom and within his or her own mind is through journaling. Journals provide teachers a tool for reflecting on their own thought processes and can also serve as a tool for students to record their thinking related to the project at hand. An example of a journal entry from Julie Russell's inquiry appears in Figure 4.7.

Strategy 6: Surveys

Some teacher-inquirers employ more formal mechanisms (such as sociograms and surveys) to capture the action, talk, thinking, and productivity that are a part of each and every school day. The most common formal mechanism we have observed in our work with teacher-inquirers is surveys. Surveys can give students a space to share their thoughts and opinions about a teaching technique or strategy, a unit, or their knowledge about particular subject matter.

Recall Brain Peters and Gail Romig's inquiry into science talks. In the excerpt below, note how the use of surveys gave Brian and Gail access to their students' thinking about their experiences during science talks:

(Text continues on page 78)

Figure 4.7   Journal Entry

Julie Russell

February 22, 2002

Inquiry Lesson #3

This week's lesson was really exciting for me because I am really beginning to
see that my efforts are making a difference. I always imagined creating a writing
atmosphere in which my students felt comfortable and confident about
presenting their work alongside that of published, established authors. In my
classroom library, I am going to have a section for "Classroom Authors" when
one of my students publishes a story, they will get a copy to take home and I will
make another copy to leave in the library. As we went around the circle and the
students named their own characters, I felt so excited for these children. They
are in an incredibly powerful creative space right now in which they feel
capable. I can remember writing my own chapter book with no hesitation when
I was eight years old. Now, I would be terrified to tackle that sort of job. I
suppose that is the source of my passion for developing writing instruction for
primary students. My dream is to help my children see themselves as "real"
authors and feel proud of their work before they begin to doubt their abilities. I
would be so proud to make a difference in that way.

I think this inquiry project has taught me a very important lesson about
pacing. One of my biggest weaknesses is expecting way too much. I know what
those expectations can do to me, and I never want to put that kind of pressure
on my children. Honestly, I think I would have done more harm than good if I
continued to push so hard. Before the writing segment of my second inquiry
lesson, the children were so excited to begin writing. When I started my third
lesson, C. actually asked, "Do we have to write a WHOLE story AGAIN?" I felt
horrible! I was so glad that we had lightened the work load. I think the whole
flow of the lesson felt better. I am a much better teacher when I do not feel
rushed and overwhelmed. I have noticed how incredibly sensitive the children
are to how I am feeling. Do you remember when I scolded them and they
apologized during that reading group? They do that often lately. They seem to
want to behave and achieve to please me, and they get upset if they think I am
not pleased. It's a big responsibility to have someone care that much about your
opinion. It becomes a constant process of reflection and negotiation, because
their sensitivity to my expectations makes me really sensitive to whether or not
my expectations are appropriate. I think that breaking the writing into more
manageable chunks made a huge difference. The children did not get burned
out, and I was able to relax and really enjoy the lesson. Part of my goal for this
project was to share my passion for writing, and I can't do that if I am not
enjoying the writing lesson.

I think that the connection to literature is very effective. Many of the
children—even those for whom writing is a struggle—are starting to include

beautiful literary language in their stories. I saw this emerge particularly during this lesson. I think the students had more time to write and I had more time to emphasize the literature. Their comments as we discussed both their fairy tales and the published fairy tales indicate that they are becoming more aware of the strategies that good authors use. One of the central ideas in my philosophy as a writing teacher is that even very young children can recognize what they like about good literature. My job as a writing teacher is to help them articulate what they like so they can begin to apply it in their own writing. It's exciting for me to see my role in writing instruction emerge, because that was one of the things I was questioning.

Upon entering into the process of using Science Talks as a means of instructing and assessing students, we were looking for answers to many questions. Could we use Science Talks as another mode of instruction? Would Science Talks enhance what we were already doing in terms of instruction? Would the use of Science Talks enable us to better assess what the students know and yet need to learn? Would Science Talks provide a vehicle for those who struggle with written forms of assessment to express their understanding meaningfully? Dickenson and Young (1998) state that science can provide "common experiences" that children can speak and write about. Would Science Talks enhance how the children communicate about these common experiences?

In addition to articulating the perspectives about Science Talks that we developed as teachers as a result of answering these questions through inquiry, we wished to discover how the students felt about the Science Talks. If the students felt comfortable and had some ownership in the activity, there may be greater participation. We used a survey which asked for information regarding the following: "What do you like about having Science Talks?", "What don't you like about Science Talks?", and "Do you have any suggestions for improving our Science Talks?"

The children's responses to this survey gleaned some interesting information and led us to the conclusion that all members of our class enjoyed Science Talks. The following two survey responses were typical of all of the responses we received:

"I like Science Talks because you might need a question answered and the teacher doesn't know the answer. With more people, more questions can be answered. I can't think of anything I don't like because science rules. I don't want to change anything 'cause things are cool as they are."

"I like Science Talks. They are cool. It is fun because we can share what we have to say. We don't even have to raise our hands."

The entire class completed the survey and not one student stated that the use of Science Talks was disliked. There were some portions of the process that were not enjoyed, and some students offered suggestions. The main item of dissatisfaction that appeared in the survey was that more than one student talked at once or that one could not speak because of others dominating the discussion. Twenty-nine percent of the class expressed this opinion.

Many students gave suggestions to improve our Science Talks. There was a desire to have smaller groups for Science Talks. One student suggested that each person in the circle have a turn and be allowed to share or pass. One child did not like the physical arrangements of the talks because she did not like sitting on the floor. Another did not like the time of day our Science Talk was held. Two students suggested that we should extend our Science Talks to other subjects . . . . We were able to learn plenty from our surveys. (Peters & Romig, 2001)

Depending on the inquiry, some teachers survey students as the first part of their investigation and have the students complete the same survey at the end of an inquiry. This is particularly useful when surveys focus on children's understandings of content or attitude toward particular components of the school day and a teacher-inquirer wishes to capture growth or change over time. Surveys can also be used in similar ways with adults.

First-grade teacher Candy Bryan and third-grade teacher Kelly Reilly-Kaminski completed a shared inquiry project that focused on understanding effective parent communication, relying on surveys as their sole form of gathering information. In the excerpt below, note the way their wondering(s) about parent communication logically led to using a survey as the main form of data collection. Also note the ways in which their data collection plan changed over time:

As a result of enrolling in a professional development course on teacher inquiry, we found the opportunity to discuss an area of concern in our classrooms. Both of us believed that parent involvement is directly related to student success in the classroom. Children will be more successful academically, complete more homework, achieve higher grades, have more positive attitudes, and behave better if parents are more involved. After all, who is a child's first and most important teacher? The answer to this question is obvious. By involving parents, teachers gain a unique perspective that provides valuable information into a child's education. According to the National PTA:

"Over 30 years' research has proven beyond dispute the positive connection between parent involvement and student success. Effectively engaging parents and families in the education of their children has the potential to be far more transformational than any other type of educational reform" (1997, p. 5).

We wondered about what methods of communication parents found valuable, what we could do to be more effective and what trends appear as students mature from the primary grades (beginning with Candy in first grade) to the intermediate grades (beginning with Kelly at third grade). At the conclusion of our research project, it was our intention to make changes to our current practices that parents would find valuable and insightful. These changes would provide parents with more information concerning their child's education and benefit all parties involved: students, parents, and teachers.

To gather the data, we needed to find out more about the parents' need for communication. We relied solely on parent surveys to gather information. We surveyed the parents once at the beginning of the project using the survey labeled Survey 1 (Figure 4.8). We asked questions about home–school journals, newsletters, and Web sites and asked for suggestions about other forms of communication that they might find useful. After reviewing the surveys we realized that we needed to ask clarifying questions. Unfortunately, the first survey was done anonymously. We were hoping to receive more honest answers if we didn't require the parents to sign the survey. This was a problem because we needed to survey some of the parents again in order to clarify their responses. We were hoping to follow-up by using short parent interviews over the phone. Instead, because we didn't know who filled out which survey, we had to survey the entire population again. In the second survey, labeled Survey 2 (Figure 4.9), we asked for the parents' preferences and suggestions about communication and participation as a volunteer in the classroom. We added the piece about participation, because of input from the first survey. We also added a few questions about e-mail as a communication tool. (Bryan & Reilly-Kaminski, 2002)

An important lesson learned about data collection from Candy and Kelly is that shifting gears midway through your inquiry, and adjusting your original plan as your inquiry unfolds, is not unusual. Originally, Candy and Kelly planned on doing one survey and follow-up phone interviews. Based on information that emerged on the first survey as well as the realization that they were unable to target particular parents with follow-up interviews because the first survey was completed anonymously, Candy and Kelly constructed a second survey.

Departing from your original data collection plan is a natural part of the inquiry process. If you find as your inquiry unfolds that forms of data collection you employed need to be adjusted—adjust accordingly! If you find as your inquiry unfolds that different forms of data collection you hadn't planned on using may be insightful to your wondering—use them! Just keep track of the decisions you make as an inquirer along the way, as articulating changes in course can also be an important piece of what you are learning.

Strategy 7: Literature as Data

Notice in the excerpts from the work of Brian and Gail and Candy and Kelly shared above that they each referenced literature connected to their wonderings and inquiry. Although we often do not think of literature as "data," it offers an opportunity to think about how your work as a teacher-inquirer is informed by and connected to the work of others. No one teaches or inquires in a vacuum. When we engage in the act of teaching, we are situated within a context (our particular classroom, grade level, school, district, state, country, etc.), and our context mediates much of what we do and understand as teachers. Similarly, when teachers inquire, their work is situated within a large, rich, preexisting knowledge base that is captured in such things as books, journal articles, newspaper articles, conference papers, and Web sites.

Looking at this preexisting knowledge base on teaching informs your study. All you need to figure out is which pieces of literature connect to your wonderings and will give you insights as your study is unfolding. Teacher-inquirers generally collect literature at two different times— (1) when they first define or are in the process of defining a wondering and (2) as their studies lead them to new findings and new wonderings. In these cases,

(Text continues on page 84)

Figure 4.8

Parent Survey 1

I will use the results of this survey to improve communication between home and school. Please fill the survey out honestly and if you have any questions, please contact me at the school.

1. What forms of communication from me do you find useful (e.g., home–school journals, newsletters, Web site, etc.)?

2. Do you read the newsletter with your child? What sections do you find the most valuable, if any? What sections are not of value to you, if any?

3. Do you have any suggestions on how I can improve the current newsletter? If so, please describe them.

4. Do you visit the classroom Web site? What components do you find the most valuable, if any? What sections are not of value to you, if any?

5. Do you have any suggestions for how I can improve the current classroom Web site? If so, please describe them.

6. Do you find home–school journals valuable? In what ways?

7. Are there any other forms of communication that you would find valuable? If so, please explain.

Figure 4.9   Parent Survey 2

Dear Parents,

I am still working on my research project about parent communication. I have some questions about home school journals and parent volunteers.

Home-school journals are journals that would be kept in your child's homework folder. They are meant to act as a two-way communication tool. If you had a question or comment to make, you could just write the note in the journal. I would read the journal and respond. I could also use it to communicate individually with parents when I have something to tell you.

Please answer Yes or No.

_____ Do you think you would use a journal like this?

_____ Do you have e-mail?

_____ Would you like to use e-mail to communicate?

If so, please provide the address. _____

_____ Would you prefer e-mail to a home-school journal?

Would you like to participate or volunteer more in the classroom?

          Yes   or   No

If you responded by circling the Yes, please check the items below that you would like to help with.

_____ Typing students' stories

_____ Helping with trips

In addition to helping with these two options, how else do you think I could use parent volunteers?

Please write your name below and return this form to school.

teachers use the literature to become well informed on what current knowledge exists in the field on their topic. Literature is an essential form of data that every teacher-inquirer should use so as to be connected to, informed by, and a contributor to the larger conversation about educational practice.

WHEN DO I COLLECT DATA AND HOW MUCH DO I COLLECT?

Now that you have seen some examples of what data collection might look like, you are ready to think about your own wondering and which forms of data collection might work for you. Unlike Candy and Kelly, who used only surveys to gain insight into their question, most teacher-inquirers find more than one data collection strategy will connect to their wondering and, subsequently, evoke more than one form of data collection in the design of their study. Using multiple sources of data can enhance your inquiry as you gain different perspectives from different strategies. In addition, by employing multiple strategies, you are able to build a strong case for your findings by pointing out the ways different data sources led you to the same conclusions. Research methodologists refer to the use of multiple data sources as "triangulation" (Cresswell, 1998; Patton, 2002). Finally, by employing multiple data sources you enhance your opportunities for learning when different data sources lead to discrepancies. It is often through posing explanations for these discrepancies that the most powerful learning of teacher inquiry occurs and that new wonderings for subsequent inquiries are generated.

As teacher-inquirers ponder the "how" of data collection and select the strategies they wish to employ, they must also ponder related questions of how long they will collect the data and how much they will collect. The "when" and "how long" of data collection is often answered by natural constraints of time imposed by such things as the length of a unit if you are doing a curriculum inquiry or the due date for your paper if engaging in inquiry as part of your student teaching or a graduate course. Optimally, data collection would proceed until you reach a state where you are no longer gaining insights into your wondering or question and no new information is emerging. This state is termed saturation by research methodologists (Creswell, 1998; Patton, 2002).

The complexities of teaching are so great, however, that in teacher research, you could be collecting data and waiting for saturation to occur indefinitely. Never drawing closure to an inquiry robs you of experiencing a process that is one of the most rewarding and exhilarating components

(Text continues on page 87)

Figure 4.10

Inquiry Brief

Beth Schickel and Darice Hampton

Purpose

As teachers in a kindergarten classroom, we interact daily with students who are at various stages of development. We have noticed that there is a wide range and varying abilities with our students when we look at phonemic awareness. Phonemic awareness is a term used to relate the awareness of phonemic units in speech to the letter symbols. We have come to realize the variance of the students through our experiences in language arts. Some students are reading and writing while others are struggling to connect letter names with letter symbols; still others are having difficulty understanding that the sounds they hear are connected to letters. This is clearly evident when one sits down to write with a student using sound spelling. As a result of these observations, we are interested in seeing the affects of supplemental phonemic awareness activities with students who are struggling in these areas.

Questions

How will small group activities with struggling students contribute to the success of their phonemic awareness and how will this affect their writing as they use sound spelling?

Subquestions

Which activities would be most helpful for the struggling students?

How much repetition is necessary before the student develops the ability to correctly identify the phonemic unit and the letter symbol?

How does the student's writing change, if at all?

Method

We will be working with two students who are having difficulty with letter and sound discrimination/recognition. Each day, one teacher will work with the students either individually or together, with concrete activities that are designed to increase their phonemic awareness. During these sessions data will be collected through note taking and observations. Student artifacts will also be collected. Although our focus is on the small group activities, the students will also be active at the writing table. They will be producing original stories through the use of sound spelling and illustration. The students will also be participating in guided reading.

Data Collection

- Observation/fieldnotes: we will take notes daily while completing

- Phonemic awareness activities

- Students' artifacts: we will collect samples of student writing and records of reading

- Daily reflection on lessons and responses from students

- Discussions with peers about daily activities and outcomes

Calendar

February

- Preassessment of students' phonemic awareness

- Data collection began through daily phonemic awareness activities

- Phonemic Awareness Inventory

- Look for patterns in data

March

- Data collection continues

- Assessment

- Begin data analysis

April

- Complete data analysis

- Prepare paper for presentation

- Continue with activities

Data Analysis

To be determined

of teacher inquiry—deeply immersing yourself in your data, articulating findings, and allowing new wonderings to emerge. Therefore, it is important that you bind your study in a particular time frame. Decisions about when and how long must be made by you as you balance what is feasible to do in the real world of your classroom and what is optimal for providing insights into your topic.

It is at this point that it is extremely valuable to develop a comprehensive plan for your inquiry. Hubbard and Power (1999) suggest that teacher-inquirers write a research brief, defined as "a detailed outline completed before the research study begins" (p. 47). A research brief may cover such aspects as the purpose of your study, your wonderings, how you will collect data, how you will analyze data (we'll explore this in the next chapter), and a time line for your study. Through the process of developing a brief, teacher-inquirers commit their energies to one idea. This commitment facilitates an inquirer's readiness to begin data collection. We end this chapter with one example of a research brief developed by Darice and Beth and two exercises you may wish to complete to help you develop your own plan—and begin!

Chapter 4 Exercises

1. Brainstorm what types of data collection strategies you might employ by creating a data collection chart. Title your chart with your main inquiry question, and generate two columns: (1) What information might help me answer my question? and (2) What data collection strategies would generate this information? An example based on Brian and Gail's work appears in Table 4.1.

Table 4.1   In What Ways Do Science Talks Enhance Student Understandings of Science Concepts?

Information That Would Help Me Answer My Question	Data Collection Strategies That Would Generate This Information
Knowing how students' conceptual knowledge develops during our astronomy unit	Collect the students' science journals
Knowing what students are saying during Science Talks	Audio taping science talks Taking fieldnotes
My thinking about what happened during the Science Talks after they occur	Teacher journal
Students' opinions about Science Talks	Surveys
Literature on Science Talks; I'm already familiar with Karen Gallas's book *Talking Their Way Into Science*	Do a search for other books or articles that are connected to science talks, building conceptual knowledge in science, teaching elementary science, and so on

2. Create your own inquiry brief that includes all of the aspects of conducting a teacher inquiry we have explored so far (e.g., won-derings and questions, collaborative support, and data collection strategies). Begin your brief with a statement that summarizes the purpose of your inquiry. End your brief with a detailed time line for completing your study.

Finding Your Findings: Data Analysis

5

Congratulations! As you begin this chapter, you are well on your way to completing your first inquiry. The good news is, with a wondering developed, a collaborative structure to support you, and data collected, you are ready to begin analyzing your data and writing up your work. This is also one of the most rewarding, exciting, thought-provoking, and growth-oriented components of inquiry!

WHAT IS DATA ANALYSIS AND HOW DO I GET STARTED?

When teacher-inquirers get to this point in their inquiries, they often ponder: "OK, I've collected all of this 'stuff' (I have a whole crate full of data)—*now* what do I do with it?" Figuring out what to do with the mounds of data that have been collected over the course of an inquiry may be quite similar to the feeling you had when you began your inquiry. Overwhelmed by the complexities inherent in teaching and the subsequent numerous possibilities for inquiry, you may have found it difficult to decide on and develop a wondering. You asked yourself, "Where do I begin?" Recall in Chapter 2 when we discussed the question of, "Where do I begin," we noted that wonderings do not materialize out of thin air. The same is true of the conclusions you draw as you near the end of a particular inquiry. Findings and conclusions do not materialize out of thin air—they come from careful scrutiny of your data as you proceed through a systematic process of making sense of what you learned.

Research methodologists have developed, described, and named a long list of systematic processes that facilitate data analysis. Two of the processes most frequently discussed in the social sciences are coding and memoing. We turn to Schwandt's (1997) *Qualitative Inquiry: A Dictionary of Terms* to provide brief, technical definitions of these concepts:

CODING—To begin the process of analyzing the large volume of data generated in the form of transcripts, fieldnotes, photographs, and the like, the qualitative inquirer engages in the activity of coding. Coding is a procedure that disaggregates that data, breaks it down into manageable segments and identifies or names those segments. . . . Coding requires constantly comparing and contrasting various successive segments of the data and subsequently categorizing them. (p. 16)

MEMOING—A procedure suggested by Barney Glaser (1978) for explaining or elaborating on the coded categories that the fieldworker develops in analyzing data. Memos are conceptual in intent, vary in length, and are primarily written to oneself. The content of memos can include commentary on the meaning of a coded category, explanation of a sense of pattern developing among categories, a ***description*** of some specific aspect of a setting or phenomenon, and so forth. Typically, the final analysis and interpretation is based on integration and analysis of memos. (pp. 89-90)

While the data analysis work of a teacher-inquirer does draw from the field of social science and borrows the processes described by these scholars, getting bogged down in the *jargon or technical language* is easy. Phrases such as "disaggregating data," "coded categories," "phenomenon," and "final analysis and interpretation" may feel foreign to your teaching practice and set up a road block to data analysis. To help you around this road block, throughout this chapter, we describe the processes of data analysis named above using language, phrases, and metaphors that are consonant with your life and work as a teacher.

In addition to the technical jargon used by researchers, baggage that we carry with us about *our own prior conceptions* of what research is can make data analysis difficult. Many people conceptualize research and analysis as quantitative "number crunching" rather than qualitative "storytelling." Frankly, good research can be either. The research method and analysis procedures needed depend on your research question. Quantitative methods may be a part of your work if you've used

Likert-scaled surveys as part of your study. However, our experience suggests that teacher questions and the resulting analysis techniques tend to be more qualitative in nature since teacher questions often seek to understand a process or the nature of a classroom phenomenon. Thus, the data analysis process we discuss in this chapter is much more inductive in nature. Even though this process may be antithetical to the ways you've thought about research (what data are and how you've analyzed data in the past), letting go of these conceptions is an essential part of beginning the data analysis process.

A final reason data analysis can appear difficult is that the inductive process you are about to enter into is *uncertain*. Many qualitative researchers we have worked with have described analysis as "murky," "messy," and "creative." To help you understand the process and scale the three hurdles to data analysis (technical jargon, prior conceptions of research, and uncertainty), we end this section by defining and describing the analysis process as a metaphorical jigsaw puzzle.

If you are a jigsaw puzzle enthusiast, a useful way to understand the process of data analysis is to imagine yourself putting together what is touted in every hobby store across the nation as the "world's most challenging puzzle." One of the reasons for this description is that the puzzle comes in a bag, not the traditional box with a cover that pictures the completed puzzle. Hence, as you work, you know that the different pieces you are putting together will result in a picture, but you are uncertain of what it is going to look like in the end. To top it off, the directions to completing this puzzle indicate that there are more pieces in your bag than you will need, and other pieces may still be at the store!

Anxious to begin the puzzle, you start the process by just spreading all of the jigsaw pieces out on your table, with no other objective than to just look at what you have. Next, you begin to assess the puzzle pieces that lie before you by pondering, "What do I notice about these pieces that might give me insights into what this puzzle is going to be?" Based on what you notice, you begin a process of grouping or sorting. Perhaps you group all the pieces by similar color (e.g., blue), thinking that all of these blue pieces might fit together to create a sky, or you group by straight edges, knowing that these will form the perimeter of the completed piece. As you actually begin fitting pieces together and the picture begins to take shape, you may realize that some of the ways you grouped the remaining puzzle pieces are not correct (i.e, "Some of these blue pieces I thought might be sky really are part of a blue boat that is taking shape in the bottom right-hand corner of the puzzle"). You regroup as you continue your work on the puzzle, creating new, additional groupings or condensing two different groupings into one.

At times the data analysis process feels overwhelming, as you may search for hours to find where one certain piece fits, only to conclude later that it is not even a part of the puzzle. Later, you realize you are missing two important pieces and subsequently must go back to the hobby store to find them. Although there are frustrations along the way, when you finally complete the puzzle, you take pride in your accomplishment.

When doing teacher inquiry and searching for what you have learned, the puzzle pieces are your data, and you are piecing your data together in different ways to create a picture of what you have learned for yourself and for others. The process is "messy," "murky," and "creative," because, just as the puzzle enthusiast must proceed without a box cover, at the start of the analysis process, you are not quite sure what this picture of your learning will look like—you must be patient as you allow your data to "speak" for itself and to lead you to your findings. Many teacher-inquirers move through the four steps of *description, sense making, interpretation,* and *implication drawing* as they analyze their data.

So what does this four-step process look like? To begin, you read and reread your entire data set, with no other objective than to get a *descriptive* sense of what you have collected. The goal of this first step of analysis is *to describe* your inquiry data using the following questions: "What did you see as you inquired?", "What was happening?", and "What are your initial insights into the data?" You might complete the description step by talking it through with another member of your inquiry community, writing it out, or choosing a combined approach and taking detailed notes as you talk.

Next, you begin the *sense-making* step by reading your entire data set and asking questions such as, "What sorts of things are happening in my data?", "What do I notice?", "How might different pieces of my data fit together?", and "What pieces of my data stand out from the rest?" To answer these questions, you may take notes in the margins of your data. You may physically cut your data apart and place the evidence in discrete piles or categories. You may decide to write down your answers to these and other questions on a separate sheet of paper, noting the location of the evidence. You may group data by using a different color marker for each theme or pattern you identify. You may highlight all excerpts from your data that fit this theme or pattern. Organizing your data is one of the most creative parts of the sense-making process.

Sometimes inquirers get stuck at this stage and need some prompts to help begin this sense-making process. Table 5.1 offers some organizing units that can serve as prompts for helping us begin our analysis. For example, you might look at your data to see if a story emerges that takes a *chronological form.* Or you may notice that your data seem to organize

Table 5.1   Examples of Organizing Units

Examples of Organizing Units		
Chronology	Key events	Various settings
People	Processes	Behaviors
Issues	Relationships	Groups
Styles	Changes	Meanings
Practices	Strategies	Episodes
Encounters	Roles	Feelings

around *key events*. Or you may see some *combination of organizing units* that is helpful. Be sure to understand that this table is by no means exhaustive and is offered just to provide some examples. As you make sense of your data, you should let the organizing units emerge from the data rather than force an external set of units. If you do decide to cut the data apart, you might want to consider keeping a complete set of data as a backup. Your answers to the description-level questions and your emerging sense-making units begin the process of grouping or sorting your data by theme or category.

Just as the jigsaw puzzle enthusiast realizes that some of the puzzle pieces are not necessary, and some are still at the store, as you analyze your data you will notice that not all of the data you collected will be highlighted/coded or will fit with your developing patterns or themes. These diverging data excerpts should be acknowledged and explained if possible. Likewise, you may find that you need to collect additional data to explore an emerging pattern. Finally, as your findings emerge, you may even regroup, rename, expand, or condense the original ways you grouped your data.

The process of sense making may take many iterations. For example, this may mean that you made data categories, named the categories, combined the named categories, renamed the categories, and eventually combined some of the combined renamed categories. As you move through this process be sure to keep track of how you arrive at the final sense making of your data. You may do this in a narrative form or you may draw a concept map for each iteration of your analysis. No matter which method you choose to map out your sense-making process—do it! The documentation will really help you as you begin the interpretive step of analysis, write up your inquiry, and discuss your findings with others.

As the puzzle nears completion and you begin the *interpretive step* of inquiry analysis, you need to construct statements that express what you learned and what the learning means. Teacher-inquirers often construct these statements by looking at the patterns that were coded and asking and answering questions such as, "What was my initial wondering and how do these patterns inform it?", "What is happening in each pattern and across patterns?", and "How are these happenings connected to . . . my teaching? . . . my students? . . . the subject matter and my curriculum? . . . my classroom/school context?"

The findings from this step can be illustrated by the teacher-inquirer in a number of ways including but not limited to the following: themes, patterns, categories, metaphors, similes, claims/assertions, typologies, and vignettes. For example, instead of describing each individual unit that Jennifer Thulin identified as she inquired into how to use music to facilitate the growth of a struggling reader, she captured the findings using the three following musical similes: "Music as a motivator," "Music as a confidence builder," and "Music as a context for making meaningful connections." Table 5.2 outlines possible illustrative techniques and provides examples.

These strategies help illustrate, organize, and communicate inquiry findings to your audience. Once you have outlined your organizing strategy, you will need to identify the data that support each finding presented in your outline. Excerpts from these data sources can be used as evidence for your claims.

Finally, upon completing each of these steps teacher-inquirers ask and answer one last set of *implication* questions as follows: (1) "What have I learned about myself as a teacher?", (2) "What have I learned about children?", (3) "What have I learned about the larger context of schools and schooling?", (4) "What are the implications of what I have learned for my teaching?", (5) "What changes might I make in my practice?", and (6) "What new wonderings do I have?"

These questions call for teacher-researchers to interpret what they have learned, to take action for change based on their study, and to generate new questions. For, unlike the puzzle enthusiast, who can marvel at the completed piece, the puzzle for a teacher-inquirer is never quite finished, even after intensive analysis. Hubbard and Power (1999) note that, "Good research analyses raise more questions than they answer" (p. 117). While you may never be able to marvel at a perfected, polished, definitive set of findings based on the data analysis from one particular inquiry, you can marvel at the enormity of what you have learned through engaging in the process and the power it holds for transforming both your identity as a teacher as well as your teaching practice. Cochran-Smith and Lytle (2001) propose that

> a legitimate and essential purpose of professional development is the development of an inquiry stance on teaching that is critical and transformative, a stance linked not only to high

Table 5.2   Strategies for Illustrating Your Findings

Themes/Patterns/Categories/Labels/Naming—A composite of traits or features; a topic for discourse or discussion; a specifically defined division; a descriptive term; set apart from others

Examples: collaboration, ownership, care, growth

Metaphors—A term that is transferred from the object it ordinarily represents to an object it represents only by implicit comparison or analogy.

"Examples: "The Illustrator," "The Translator," "The Reporter," "The Guide," and "Casting the Play"

Simile—Two unlike things are compared, often in a phrase introduced by "like" or "as"

Examples: "music as a motivator," "music as a confidence builder," "music as a context for making meaningful connections," and "writing as conversation"

Claims/Assertions—A statement of fact or assertion of truth.

Example: "Inappropriate expectations discouraged many of the learners in my classroom and hindered my effectiveness as a writing teacher."

Typologies—A systematic classification of types (Patton)

Examples: Different uses for puppets—instructional, entertainment, therapeutic

Vignettes—A brief descriptive literary sketch (ELY)

Examples: "The Struggle for Power; Who is in Control"

The children were engaged in conversation at the meetings, jobs were continuing to get done, but there was still a struggle centering around who was in control. With the way the class decided to make a list of jobs, break the jobs up into groups, choose the people they wanted to work with, there were breaks in communication. Conflicts were arising with the groups. Everyone was mostly aiming to get "their own" way.

standards for the learning of all students but also to social change and social justice and to the individual and collective growth of teachers. (p. 46)

After completing data analysis, marvel at your growth and the impact you can have as an individual teacher who has joined a larger community of teacher-researchers. Through engagement in inquiry as a member of this community, you are contributing to the transformation of the teaching profession!

WHAT MIGHT DATA ANALYSIS LOOK LIKE?

To exemplify the process of data analysis we just described, we turn to the first piece of teacher inquiry completed by veteran teacher-researcher

Amy Ruth (Ruth, 1999, 2001, 2002). Recall that Amy completed her first teacher inquiry as an intern in a professional development school by looking closely at an individual English as a Second Language Learner she called "Adam." Amy was particularly interested in learning about the ways peer interaction facilitated Adam's written language development.

To gain insights into her wondering, Amy collected data in three ways over a two-month time period. Amy's first mode of data collection was her own taking of fieldnotes. She developed a data collection sheet to complete each time she worked with Adam at the writing center. On the data sheet, Amy diagrammed the seating arrangement to keep track of where group members chose to sit each time they came to the writing center. Next on the data collection sheet, Amy had a space for observations. In this space, Amy noted anything that stood out to her during the time Adam's group was at the center. There was also a place on the data collection sheet labeled Notable Dialogue where she scripted comments that occurred between peers during their interactions. Finally, Amy had a place labeled Additional Comments where she noted anything else occurring during time at the writing center that was interesting or intriguing.

Amy's second mode of data collection was to keep a personal journal on each day that she met Adam's group at the writing center. Amy notes, "These entries helped me to gather my thoughts, ideas, and further questions concerning my initial wonderings" (Ruth, 1999, p. 7). Finally, one of us, as Amy's supervisor, scripted notes of interactions at the writing center while Amy taught.

After two months of collecting data in these three forms, Amy approached the almost-filled-to-the-top box in which she was keeping all of this data, plus articles and books she had found on the writing process and ESL students. She set aside a few hours on a Saturday morning to begin the process of creating a picture of what she had learned. To begin, she took each piece of data out of the box and organized them chronologically beginning with the first piece collected and ending with the last, and read through every piece. By reading through her entire data set, Amy was reminded of incidents that occurred throughout the duration of her inquiry (through her own fieldnotes and those scripted by her supervisor), as well as her thoughts about Adam, peer interaction, and the writing process as her inquiry unfolded (through her journal entries). In addition, reviewing readings that had appeared in such journals as *Journal of Second Language Writing* and *TESOL Journal* contributed to Amy's developing understanding of her work with Adam. The process of reading the data set in its entirety "freshened up" and provided a description of all that Amy had been thinking about and doing for the past two months.

With all she had collected fresh in her mind, Amy read through the entire data set a second time. On this second time through, Amy began

Figure 5.1   Amy's List of "What I'm Noticing"

Themes?   4/99

Inquiry → what I'm Noticing

Adam - asks B. to draw pictures. Directs B. w/ descriptive words. B. draws for him, asking questions (clarifying questions

Small group - K. A. & S. do a lot of small talk w/ K - I'm noticing how much more she has to say about her story than what's on page

am class - more independent writers

K. - eager to share w/ me, but not peers

S. - so artistically centered w/ drawings (little written) ? my question: How is crafting (cutting + gluing) tied to writing?

B. - did not want to write words till peer suggestion made

Adam & B. - still requesting B. to draw particular animals for him → Adam draws w/ him simultaneously → upon urging, Adam & B. will write out words on paper.

---

sense making. As she read she asked herself, "What am I noticing about my data?" She constructed a list as she read titled "Inquiry—What I'm Noticing" (see Figure 5.1).

From looking at this list, Amy decided that her next step was to read the data again, but, this time through, to focus solely on Adam and her initial wondering, stated as, "How does peer interaction facilitate Adam's writing at the kindergarten writing center?" She wrote this question on an index card and laid it in front of her to remind her of what she was looking for in this third read of her entire data set. This time, she decided to mark her data by highlighting any pieces of it that pertained to this question in pink.

Once this process was completed, Amy took a break for lunch and then returned to her data for a fourth reading. During this fourth sweep, however, Amy read only what had been highlighted in pink. Through reading only the pink data excerpts, she generated a list of seven patterns that seemed to describe and capture the essence of what was occurring over and over in her data. She named each of these patterns as follows: (1) Requesting Drawings From Peers, (2) Adam's Verbalization as Drawing Object, (3) Labeling Objects Around the Room, (4) Outgoing Personality, (5) Role Taking in Group, (6) Burdens Others, and (7) Asking for Clarification.

Next, Amy created a coding mechanism for each of her named patterns, creating a symbol that corresponded to each pattern (i.e., a "tree" corresponded to pattern 1, a "bubble" corresponded to pattern 2, the word *dog* corresponded to pattern 3, a "smiley face" corresponded to pattern 4, a "hat" corresponded to pattern 5, a "sad face" corresponded to pattern 6, and a "check" corresponded to pattern 7). Just as Amy had done previously when she wrote her question on an index card and laid it in front of her to remind her of what she was looking for as she read, Amy noted each pattern and symbol on an index card and kept this card in front of her as she read through the entire data set a fifth time. This time through, she underlined and used her symbols to code the data. Amy's index card denoting the pattern symbols, as well as one piece of coded data from each of the three ways it was collected, appear in Figures 5.2 to 5.5.

A few days later, Amy sorted her data by pattern, reading through only the excerpts that pertained to each pattern that was coded. As she read through each pattern, she began the interpretive step of analysis. She asked herself, "What is happening in each pattern?", "How are the patterns connected to each other?", and "What do these patterns mean in relation to my initial wondering?" This time through, Amy noted the ways some patterns were connected to each other. For example, Amy saw connections between the four categories: (1) Adam's outgoing personality, (2) requests for drawings from peers, (3) different roles at the writing center, and (4) burdening others. She regrouped her data accordingly.

That week, Amy talked with her own peers at a seminar about what she was seeing. As she talked about the patterns, Amy noted that aspects of who Adam was as a person and learner that were strong attributes (i.e., Adam had an outgoing personality and Adam was acquiring more and more spoken English words) were positive forces in the development of his writing. Adam was able to use his personality and the blossoming of his spoken English language as critical aids to his progress as a writer by asking peers for help, especially the child who had taken on the role of artist

Figure 5.2   Amy's Index Card Denoting Symbols Used for Coding

in the group. Amy noted that requests for drawing from the group's artist were frequent in her data and were appropriate and productive for Adam. As Adam's request for drawing from the child who took on the role of artist at the writing center became more frequent, the artist became reluctant to respond to Adam's requests. Amy shared with her colleagues incidences that appeared in her data such as the following:

> Adam said, "Books! Draw books." The artist replied, "Books? I can draw one book." Adam held up three fingers and replied, "No, three books." The artist shook his head no. Adam said again, "Four? Four books." The artist drew just one book, and eventually, Adam drew the rest.

In talking about her data, Amy also shared that what she had coded as a burden for the child who took on the role of the artist also seemed to lead that same child to become more immersed in his own writing. Amy shared that as the inquiry proceeded, the artist seemed more interested in doing his own writing and drawing. His own stories were growing more elaborate, and it appeared that he was trying to spend more time and effort on his own stories.

Figure 5.3   Example of Coded Data—Journal

Amy Ruth

Inquiry Journal

Tuesday, March 2, 1999

After finally deciding to concentrate my inquiry focus on "Adam", a ESL student, I have really started concentrating on his interactions and writing at the Writing Table during Lang Arts centers. I am curious about how his interactions with peers will *Initial Question* influence, encourage, and help the progress and growth of his writing. Lately, Adam has been asking peers (B., in particular) to draw objects on his paper for him. Mostly everyone in the classroom knows that B. is particularly skilled and practiced at drawing dinosaurs and whales. They were the first two animals that I witnessed Adam requesting. Adam also goes as far as to tell B. what colors he would like things to be. After B. draws the request, Adam then adds details to the picture, usually talking as he does so. For example: a dinosaur drawn by B. and then Adam added a tree that the dinosaur was eating. Adam verbalized "tree" and eating sounds as he drew.

It is particularly interesting to see Adam requesting drawings by his peers, due to the use of the English language that we have seen really emerging recently. Within the past month we have seen tremendous growth in Adam's use of vocabulary. He is formulating longer sentences and is very eager to share his ideas through words now. I have noticed that he is more interested in full group activities in which he may have the chance to share his ideas. He raises his hand frequently, and volunteers many answers.

I am interested in seeing how this begins to play out in his writing. I am beginning to think of strategies that will encourage him to add words to his drawings.

Through engaging in dialogue, Amy's colleagues helped her capture what she was learning in a single statement or assertion: "A productive tension exists between Adam, his personality, his oral language development and the ways he uses these attributes in interactions with peers at the writing center."

Figure 5.4   Example of Coded Data—Fieldnotes Taken by Amy

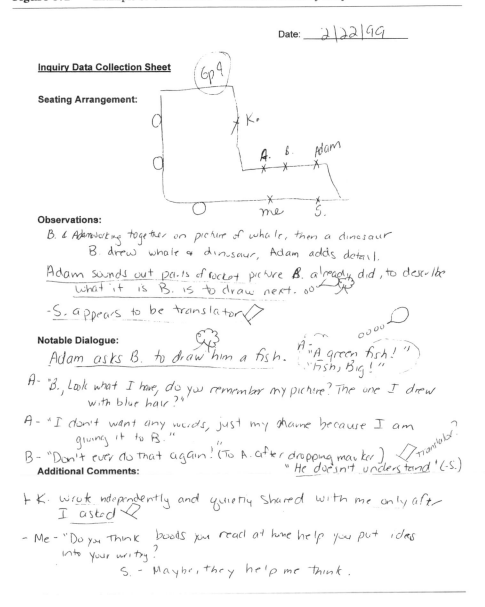

Date: 2/22/99

Inquiry Data Collection Sheet   Gp 4

Seating Arrangement:

K.

A. B. Adam

me S.

Observations:

B. & Adam working together on picture of whale, then a dinosaur.
   B. drew whale & dinosaur, Adam adds detail.

Adam sounds out parts of rocket picture B. already did, to describe
   what it is B. is to draw next.

-S. appears to be translator

Notable Dialogue:

Adam asks B. to draw him a fish.   A- "A green fish!"   "fish, Big!"

A- "B., look what I have, do you remember my picture? The one I drew
      with blue hair?"

A- "I don't want any words, just my name because I am
      giving it to B."

B- "Don't ever do that again! (To A. after dropping marker)   Translator?
      Additional Comments: "He doesn't understand" (-S.)

+ K. wrote independently and quietly shared with me only after
    I asked

- Me - "Do you think books you read at home help you put ideas
    into your writing?
          S. - Maybe, they help me think.

Fitting together these four different patterns revealed to Amy the complex nature and delicate balance of the interactions that were occurring at the writing center. Through her inquiry and data analysis, Amy gained new understandings of what was occurring—understandings that would never have emerged in the absence of systematic study. Amy used the new knowledge she had constructed to make adjustments in her teaching and navigate the productive tension between Adam and the artist in the

Figure 5.5   Example of Coded Data—Fieldnotes Scripted by Supervisor

③

Gives children reminders at the project table. "It is almost time for me to knock."

Transition

- Amy knocks - Children line up to switch centers. She waits for all children, gives some individual reminders and knocks.

Center Rotation #2

- "How do you stay healthy?"
- Mentor arrives at project table.

Amy at Writing Table (INQUIRY)

- A. talking to children about O circles-globe "DOG"
- Children say that "It is one of A.'s words."
- A. gets up and spins the globe.
- "Miss Ruth" - A. gets Amy's attention. He points again to globe
- Amy asks A to draw some of those countries. He hands paper to little girl across from him.
- "K. needs to work on her story too."
- A. not working - looking around room, back to globe.
- "A. be careful! Come and add some more on here.
- Amy moves over to direct A.'s writing. A. knows some but not all sounds. He has difficulty find the "T" even when Amy tells him. Someone helps him with "R" Two other children are huddled over the alphabet list. They are trying to help.

room by increasing her own interactions with Adam, but still allowing for peer interactions to continue:

I did not want Adam's requests and demands to hold back his peer's writing, although I still believe that those interactions were important for the progress of both children's writing. I tried to hold more of my own conversations with Adam, posing questions to him about his drawings, and assisting him whenever possible with words he would use to label his drawings. (Ruth, 1999, p. 10)

The completed picture of Amy's learning and what that learning meant for her practice was taking shape through data analysis.

At this time in the data analysis process, Amy abandoned her initial wondering and generated a new wondering: "What does writing mean to Adam?" Amy continued to analyze her data and collect more data over the next few weeks with this question in mind. At the close of her data analysis, Amy reflected as follows:

> It is very exciting to look over the themes I found, and to realize that there was something very important going on with Adam and his peers at the writing center! Had I not posed the original question, I may never have really noticed what it was that was actually occurring. I now know how important the process of collecting data is. My data and themes did not necessarily definitively answer my initial question. But more importantly, they allowed me to see what was really growing and developing at our kindergarten writing center. Plus, I answered an entirely new question!
>
> I have found out, through this inquiry project, that there really are not any concrete answers to the initial question. It is where the initial question leads that is important. The initial question allowed me to open up to seeing, hearing, and experiencing all that was going on at the writing table. I let the data collection and analysis lead me to my findings, instead of me leading the data collection and analysis to what I was hoping to find. (Ruth, 1999, pp. 12-13)

As you reflect on Amy's example of data analysis, remember the three words we used to describe the data analysis process: "messy," "murky," and "creative." With this in mind, realize that your particular data analysis might not proceed exactly as Amy's. Every teacher is unique, every inquiry is unique, and, hence, every piecing together of the inquiry data to create a picture of the learning that has occurred is unique. Yet, as you finish this chapter, you now have knowledge of a common set of general procedures utilized to analyze data and a sense of how those general procedures may play out in a particular teacher-inquirer's work.

You may wish to complete additional studies of the data analysis process before you begin or as you engage in the process yourself. We conclude this chapter with suggested exercises for data analysis, as well as a list of references you may find useful as you engage in this most difficult, but most rewarding, component of inquiry.

Exercise 1

The first step of analysis is *to describe* your inquiry. Read through your data carefully. Take notes as your read. After reading your data, respond to the following questions:

- What did you see as you inquired?
- What was happening?
- What are your initial insights into the data?

Exercise 2

The second step of analysis is to begin *making sense of* your data. The organizing units presented in Table 5.1 can serve as prompts for helping you begin your analysis.

1. Use the chart to help you identify or construct possible organizing units for your data. Be sure to consider organizing units that emerge from within your inquiry.
2. Now take a stab at organizing your data and identifying the units of analysis that emerge in your inquiry data. For example, maybe the important story in your data involves "changes" and you identify categories such as "changes for kids," "changes in content," and "changes in instruction."

Exercise 3

Once you have a general idea of the important units of data and an idea of the emerging story, you need to decide how you will present the data. Read through the list of strategies presented in Table 5.2; they are designed to help you illustrate your *interpretive* findings. Remember, this is by no means an exhaustive list.

1. Now, you will need to choose a strategy or strategies for illustrating and organizing your own findings for your audience. Once again, use your creativity to organize your thoughts.
2. Outline the elements of your organizing strategy and identify the data that you will use to support each component of your outline.

Exercise 4

You probably thought the most difficult step of the analysis process was completed. However, the final *implications* step remains. Your remaining responsibility is to move from interpretation of the findings that you present in Exercise 3 to articulating the implications or "So What?" of your study. Some helpful questions follow that may prompt your thinking in this area:

- What have I learned about myself as a teacher?
- What have I learned about children?
- What are the implications of my findings for the content I teach?
- What have I learned about the larger context of schools and schooling?
- What are the implications of what I have learned for my teaching?
- What changes might I make in my own practice?
- What new wonderings do I have?

Additional References for Inquiry Analysis

Creswell, J. W. (1998). *Qualitative inquiry and research design: Choosing among five traditions.* Thousand Oaks, CA: Sage.

Glanz, J. (1998). *Action research: An educational leader's guide to school improvement.* Norwood, MA: Christopher-Gordon.

Marshall, C., & Rossman, G. B. (1999). *Designing qualitative research* (3rd ed.). Thousand Oaks, CA: Sage.

Patton, M.Q. (2002). *Qualitative researcher and evaluation methods* (3rd ed.). Thousand Oaks, CA: Sage.

Strauss, A., & Corbin, J. (1998). *Basics of qualitative research.* Thousand Oaks, CA: Sage.

Wolcott, H. F. (1994). *Transforming qualitative data: Description, analysis, and interpretation.* Thousand Oaks, CA: Sage.

Stringer, E. T. (1996). *Action research: A handbook for practitioners.* Thousand Oaks, CA: Sage.

Extending Your Learning: The Inquiry Write-Up

6

You have just completed the process of data analysis during which time you sorted, re-sorted, and made sense of all you had collected throughout the duration of your inquiry project. You thought about your inquiry as a whole. You thought about what was happening in the data. You thought about what you learned. You thought about the implications of what you learned for your own teaching practice. In short, you did a lot of thinking!

A wonderful way to *think* about your inquiry is to *write*. Noted educational ethnographer Harry Wolcott (1990) goes so far as to state that writing and thinking are synonymous: "The conventional wisdom is that writing reflects thinking. I am drawn to a different position: Writing *is* thinking" (p. 21). Referring specifically to the process of teacher inquiry, Mills (2003) further states that there is great value in writing up research because,

> the very process of writing requires the writer to clarify meaning—choose words carefully, thoughtfully describe that which is experienced or seen, reflect on experiences, and refine phrasing when putting words on a page. You may learn something very important about your students and their learning—something you may have missed had you not considered your words on the page—as you formally write about your research. (p. 164)

For this reason, we recommend writing as an extension of data analysis and as a wonderful way to extend your learning.

WHY SHOULD I WRITE?

Unfortunately, while writing is a terrific mechanism for clarifying thinking as you summarize what you have learned and for giving your learning a form that can be shared with others, writing is not a part of a teacher's daily work, and it takes a great deal of time. Mills (2003) suggests challenging the time constraint by making writing a part of your professional life and responsibility. Mills suggests capturing the minutes and hours—before school; after school; during preparation periods; or in lieu of canceled faculty meetings, failed parent conferences, and "sit-and-get" professional development days. When all else fails, use personal time to get writing done.

If you can get past the time constraint and the resistance to engaging in an activity that Wolcott describes at its best as "always challenging and sometimes satisfying" (p. 12), we believe that the times that it is satisfying will outweigh all the difficulty and frustration inherent in writing, and that through the writing process, you will take your own individual inquiry to a new level. Mills (2003) suggests sound reasons for writing. We end this section with his four most compelling reasons to write:

> *Clarification*—Writing your research requires clarity and accuracy of expression. Writing about your research activities encourages thought and reflection, and perhaps creates new questions that are resolved, which shape and complete your research.

> *Empowerment*—Reflecting on your practices through writing will empower you to continue to challenge the status quo and be an advocate for your children.

> *Generative*—Writing is a generative activity that culminates in a product, something tangible that you can share with colleagues, supervisors, and parents.

> *Accomplishment*—Writing up your research will provide you with a sense of accomplishment. It is both humbling and exciting when colleagues read your work and compliment you on your accomplishments! (pp. 164-165)

WHAT MIGHT MY WRITING LOOK LIKE?

If you recall, Julie Russell was passionate about writing and this passion led to her inquiry into second graders' writing. Julie's passion for writing makes her a logical teacher-inquirer to feature in this chapter as an example of what your work may look like in a written form. Julie's work provides only one example of "the look" of an inquiry write-up. We encourage you to view other write-ups as models, such as journals that publish teacher inquiries and action research Web sites. While Julie's work is but one example, we select it for the poignant way she developed four critical features of any write-up: (1) providing background information, (2) sharing the design of the inquiry (procedures, data collection, and data analysis), (3) stating the learning and supporting the statements with data, and (4) providing concluding thoughts.

Step 1: Providing Background Information

A strong way to begin your writing is to provide background information. Sharing your context, what led you to this particular study, how it is connected to others' thinking about the topic of your inquiry, and what processes you used to gain insights into a particular wondering provide a foundation for your audience to understand your work and to make judgments as to its transferability to their own teaching situation. Here, we reprint Julie's introduction to her work that was previously shared as an example of finding your wondering at the intersection of your personal and professional identities in Chapter 2. This time, as you read this excerpt, notice how Julie helped the reader understand who she was as a teacher and person ("My goal as a teacher is to help children become lifelong learners who can think critically about the world around them and create and articulate their own ideas"), what was occurring in her own classroom ("Some children wrote independently and produced several pages of text during each workshop. Others wrote one sentence at a time and frequently approached me to ask, "Am I done yet?"), what was occurring in the field ("As I studied children's writing development, I realized that the range of writing behaviors in my classroom were common"), what was occurring in her district ("My mentor spoke to many of the children about meeting the district's benchmark for writing by the end of the school year"), and what was occurring in her own teaching ("I began to doubt my ability to provide my students with writing instruction that would help them meet the district's writing goals and that would inspire them to enjoy writing"). Through her writing, Julie shows how all of these components coalesced to lead to this particular inquiry:

I can still remember every detail of the moment when I became a writer. The warm August air sticks to my skin, powdery chalk dust tickles my nose, and the comforting sounds of my mother making dinner fill my ears whenever I begin to put words on a page. I found my voice as a writer the summer before second grade. I was six years old, and my older sister had suddenly decided that she was too mature to play with me. She would disappear with her friends, and I was left to fill the long, summer days without her. One afternoon, I wandered into the basement and started to draw on an old chalkboard that my sister and I used when we were "playing school." After a while, I stopped drawing and began writing poetry. When my mother called me for dinner, she saw my poems and became my first audience. She encouraged my efforts and gave me a small, yellow notebook so I could continue to write. My passion for writing grew as I continued to read quality literature and experienced the powerful ways in which expert authors manipulate language and develop engaging stories. Throughout my life, I have turned to written words to express my thoughts and ideas.

As I developed a teaching philosophy, I realized that my passion for teaching is intertwined with my passion for writing. My goal as a teacher is to help children become lifelong learners who can think critically about the world around them and create and articulate their own ideas. I hope that, by sharing my love for writing with my students, I can help them express the thoughts and opinions that are important and meaningful to them. Therefore, when I pictured my future classroom, I always seemed to arrive during writer's workshop. I assumed that I would be an effective, engaging writing teacher simply because I enjoyed writing. I imagined a classroom filled with eager students who loved writing and could not wait to commit their ideas to paper. I was thrilled to be an intern in a second grade classroom, because I could remember the wonderful writing experiences I had during my own second grade year.

As I began my internship experience, I helped provide writing instruction for a group of second graders with differing strengths, needs, and interests. I quickly realized that teaching writing is extremely complicated. Some children wrote independently and produced several pages of text during each workshop. Others wrote one sentence at a time and frequently approached me to ask, "Am I done yet?" I often sat with a small group of students who struggled to get their thoughts down on paper. As I tried to keep these children on task and encourage them to continue writing, I asked questions and made story maps. At the end of many writing sessions, I felt uncomfortable with the amount of support I was giving to some young writers. Several children who were quite capable of writing independently often came to me and asked, "Can I write with you?" I worried that I was allowing some children to become too dependent on my help and my influence was hindering the flow of their ideas.

As I studied children's writing development, I realized that the range of writing behaviors in my classroom was common for second graders. I felt relief when I read the experts' descriptions of second grade writers and they mirrored my feelings about the young writers in my classroom. Some children write "fluently" and approach writing with "carefree confidence" (Calkins, 1986, p. 67). These children write long, detailed narratives with ease. Other children seem to erase more than they write. Second graders are beginning to become "aware of an audience" for their writing, and the "easy confidence" they felt as first graders often turns into their first cases of "writer's block" (Calkins, 1986, p. 68). They are concerned about approaching tasks in the "right way," and that vulnerability makes writing a difficult and painstaking process for many children (Calkins, 1986, p. 69). Therefore, writing instruction in second grade must address this wide range of writing behaviors.

During the students' goal-setting conferences in the beginning of the school year, my mentor, Linda Witmer, spoke to many of the children about working toward meeting the district's benchmark for writing by the end of the year. According to this benchmark, the students must be able to write stories with beginnings, middles, and endings. These stories should be understandable and must include characters, settings, and major events. The students are also expected to include some descriptive language, use some punctuation and capitalization, and spell the district benchmark words correctly. The students must complete the writing assessment independently. After winter break, Linda and I were both concerned about our students' writing. As I looked through the students' work, I noticed that extremely capable children were often scoring below the benchmark. Many of the children were still writing incomplete stories, and endings were particularly difficult for many students. Although our students had wonderful, creative ideas, we worried that several of them would not meet the district's benchmark for writing because they did not take the reader on a complete journey from beginning to middle to end.

My initial experiences as a writing teacher were frustrating. After years of imagining myself as an effective writing teacher, I was dismayed when I realized that my efforts were not helping my students meet their writing goals. In some cases, I worried that I was doing more harm than good because my attempts to help often became persistent prompting that drowned out the students' voices in their own writing. I was heartbroken when students resisted writing, because I was so eager to share my passion for stories and language. When I conducted a survey to collect data about the students' attitudes toward writing, I was concerned when I realized that many children thought that they were good writers because of "neat handwriting," "good spelling," or "using time wisely." Although those skills are important, I noticed that most children did not mention that they were proud of their ability to create stories. Gradually, I began to doubt my ability to provide my students with writing instruction that would help them meet the district's writing goals and that would inspire them to enjoy writing. My passion for writing, which I believed would be an asset in the classroom, actually hindered my progress as a writing teacher because I struggled to relate to and communicate with students who resisted writing. As I studied writing instruction, I learned that a teacher's personal experiences with the subject matter influences the way he/she teaches his/her students (Frank, 1979). I realized that, because I had positive writing experiences as a child, I naively assumed that all of my second graders would react to writing with similar enthusiasm.

My passion for writing and teaching, as well as my frustrations about the realities of teaching writing, led me to my wonderings. I wanted to do a project that would focus on my students' development as writers and would also help me develop as a writing teacher. Therefore, I began my project with the following wonderings:

Will my second graders write more complete stories if the elements of a story are broken down into a series of mini-lessons?

Will my second graders become more independent writers and gain confidence in their writing abilities if my expectations for their writing are more explicit?

Will collaborating with other learners help my students grow as writers?

Will my students grow as writers if the lessons include opportunities to make connections between children's literature and their own stories?

Will these changes in writing instruction improve the way my students feel about themselves as writers and the way I feel about myself as a writing teacher? (Russell, 2002)

This lengthy excerpt from Julie's inquiry provides contextualization for the audience, and this contextualization prepares the audience to understand Julie's particular approach to her work.

Step 2: Sharing the Design of the Inquiry (Procedures, Data Collection, and Data Analysis)

A key feature that sets inquiry apart from the daily reflection that teachers engage in is that it is conducted in a systematic, intentional way.

Hence, sharing your system (what you did), as well as your intentions (how you did what you did: data collection and analysis), is important. In the next excerpt, notice how Julie discusses her instructional plan for this inquiry and the ways she collected data. Also notice how she articulates the ways that data collection and analysis interacted with each other as her plan of action for instruction changed over time:

Once I developed my wonderings, I began studying both primary students' writing development and methods for writing instruction. I read resource books written by primary teachers that included actual lesson plans and anecdotes about students and their writing. I also read books by researchers who focused more on theories about writing development. I looked through my students' portfolios to learn about the problems they faced when they were writing stories. My students completed a survey that focused on their attitudes toward writing and about themselves as writers.

As I began my project, the primary division at my school was beginning the "Land of Make-Believe" unit. The unit fit well with my wonderings because it is language arts-intensive and it includes many examples of quality children's literature. I used some fairy tales from the unit as well as stories that were recommended in my other resources to develop a series of five literature-based mini-lessons. As I developed my lessons, I often referred to Susan Lunsford's (1998) *Literature-Based Mini-Lessons to Teach Writing*. Lunsford advocates using children's literature to teach writing because the literature gives students examples of how expert authors deal with the problems that all writers face. I wanted my students to feel that they were capable, valuable members of a community of writers that includes published authors. I hoped that, by using quality children's literature in my lessons, I would be able to have discussions with my students about effective writing. Once the strategies in the literature were articulated, I hoped that the children would begin to apply them in their own stories.

Initially, I planned to teach lessons about character, setting, problem, solution, and complete stories. Each lesson followed the same basic format. As a large group, the students and I read and discussed sections of children's literature that exemplified the story element we were studying. We brainstormed ideas that the students could use in their own writing. Then, the students were expected to apply the story element we studied by writing their own stories. I prepared rubrics for each story element. The rubrics were designed so that the writer, a peer, and a teacher could evaluate the way the writer used a particular story element in his/her story. I also scored the stories using the District's rubric so that the students and I could monitor our progress toward the benchmark for second grade.

As I interacted with the children and looked at my data, I changed some aspects of my lessons based on my developing understandings of effective writing instruction and second graders' needs and abilities. After my first two workshops, I was extremely dissatisfied with my project. When I began the setting workshop, one child asked, "Do we have to write a whole story AGAIN?" The students' reluctance to write disturbed me, because I was so anxious to help them enjoy and look forward to writing. The class discussion at the beginning of the setting workshop was also quite discouraging for me because the children did not remember the concepts we studied during the character workshop the week before. When I planned the workshops, I intended to help the students build a concept of a complete story by studying one element at a time. For this plan to work, the students had to transfer the concepts from one workshop to the next. After discussing my concerns with my mentor and my supervisor, I decided to back up and change the structure of the workshops. I planned three workshops on beginnings, middles, and endings, and then a final workshop on complete stories. During the beginning, middle, and ending workshops, the students only needed to write the story element we discussed on that particular day. This change shortened the students' writing time to about twenty minutes and made the workshops more focused and less stressful. During the final workshop, the students were expected to put all of the elements together and write complete stories without assistance.

I also changed the types of collaboration that took place during my lessons. During the first two workshops, I allowed the students to find their own partners when they were done writing. When my data indicated that this arrangement was disorganized and ineffective, I decided to assign partners. Linda, my mentor, suggested that I create partnerships of students with similar writing abilities. I also increased the amount of collaboration in each lesson. The students began to work with their partners as they brainstormed before writing and as they evaluated their work after writing.

Initially, I took full responsibility for writing the rubrics and setting the expectations for our writing activities. I provided the checklists for the first five workshops. As I examined my data, researched writing instruction, and spoke with my mentor and my supervisor, I began to wonder about the potential impact of having the students help set their own expectations. Therefore, during the class discussion for the fifth writer's workshop, I asked the students to list the qualities that a complete story needed. This list became the rubric for the complete stories the students created during the final workshop. This change in my original plan allowed me to compare and contrast my expectations for the students with the students' expectations for themselves.

Throughout this project, I tried to reinforce concepts from writer's workshop during reading instruction. During the "Land of Make-Believe" unit, I was reading fairy tales with a group of eleven children. I encouraged the students to reflect upon the authors' decisions. The students responded to questions about characters, settings, problems or adventures, and endings. We talked about elements of the stories that were effective and elements that were not satisfying for us as readers. The students also had opportunities to study the authors' word choices. We searched for descriptive language in the texts and discussed the ways that these "dazzling words" affected readers.

Throughout the workshops, I took notes about the students' behaviors, my supervisor scripted class discussions, and I wrote journal entries about each lesson. These texts provided me with data about my students' growth as writers and my growth as a writing teacher. After the series of writer's workshops, I gave the students the same survey that they had completed before the workshops to collect data about their attitudes toward writing and about themselves as writers. I compared the pre-surveys and the post-surveys and looked for changes in the students' opinions. I also interviewed four children who had different writing abilities and styles to learn more about their reactions to various aspects of the writer's workshops. Finally, I looked at the students' work to determine whether or not my lessons had been effective. As I examined my data, several claims about writing and writing instruction emerged.

Step 3: Stating the Learning and Supporting the Statements With Data

With detailed knowledge of the "how" of the inquiry, the audience is now ready to understand Julie's findings, which she presents as "claims." As Julie engaged in the process of writing this report of her inquiry, she clarified her thinking by choosing words and phrases that carefully reflect and represent her learnings in this form. As Julie began writing and developing each claim, she also realized that her claims could be organized into four conceptual categories. She did a lot of cutting and pasting as she organized and reorganized for the reader. In the absence of the process of writing it up, Julie would not have taken her work to this organizational level and not realized the extent of her own learning. The four categories and claims associated with each category that she generated as she wrote about her work included the following:

Category 1: Student Growth

Claim 1: The series of six writer's workshops that focused on the parts of stories helped several of my second graders write stories that reached the district benchmark for writing.

Category 2: Setting Expectations

Claim 2: Inappropriate expectations discouraged many of the learners in my classroom and hindered my effectiveness as a writing teacher.

Claim 3: My students were my most valuable resource as I created developmentally appropriate expectations.

Claim 4: Rubrics were helpful for some students, but they were not effective for other students.

Category 3: Collaboration

Claim 5: Collaborating with others helped some students develop ideas and grow as writers.

Claim 6: Other students found that collaborating was ineffective for them as writers.

Category 4: Connections to Literature

Claim 7: Students who make connections between writing and literature can use literature to help them solve problems when they are writing.

Claim 8: Students who are immersed in literature incorporate more literary language in their writing.

Claim 9: Students who read from a writer's perspective are comfortable thinking critically about literature.

Claim 10: The students in Room 20 are members of a writing community that included published authors.

In the next passage from Julie's inquiry write-up, notice how Julie states each of these claims and builds an argument to support her claim by providing evidence with excerpts and vignettes from her data. When you write, in essence, you are building an argument that is not unlike a district attorney's building a case to prosecute a defendant. A case built on only one piece of evidence would never go to trial. The attorney must piece together a string of evidence to create a strong case. The same is true for a teacher-inquirer. In presenting and sharing findings, the teacher-inquirer pieces together a string of evidence to support statements of his or her learning. The case is stronger when evidence is provided from multiple sources (what we learned in Chapter 4 is referred to by research methodologists as triangulation). As you read, notice how Julie weaves data excerpts from multiple sources (scripted fieldnotes by her supervisor, her own journal entries, student work, student surveys, interviews, and literature about children's writing) throughout the discussion of each claim.

Student Growth

The series of six writer's workshops that focused on the parts of stories helped several of my second graders write stories that reached the district benchmark for writing.

As I looked through the students' portfolios at the beginning of my project, I noticed that the students who were scoring below the benchmark were not writing complete stories. They often had creative ideas and wonderful language, but they did not include crucial parts of the story. Endings were, by far, the most difficult story element for my students. Many children seemed to grow tired by the time they reached the end of their stories. They would write a few quick sentences that did not explain how the problem was solved just so they could be done. Other children had difficulty organizing their thoughts. They would write down their ideas without planning their stories, so their plots were scattered and their endings were not related to the rest of their stories.

As I planned the writing activity for the first workshop, I used my mentor's guidance to make the task similar to the district's writing assessment. After our read-aloud and our discussion about characters, I gave the students two titles. Each child had to choose one of the titles and write a story based on the title they chose. This writing activity was independent. The children had to work quietly and write their entire stories in one session.

When I scored these stories using the district's rubric, my data were consistent with my observations of the students' portfolios. Seventeen of my 18 second graders were present and wrote stories during our first writer's workshop. Of those 17 children, 11 scored below the district's benchmark because their stories were incomplete. As I looked through my comments on the stories, I noticed that 10 of the 11 stories that did not reach the benchmark lacked endings. Several stories also needed more detail in the middle to make the problems or adventures interesting and understandable.

During our sixth and final writer's workshop, the students were expected to put all of the elements of a story together. Their complete stories were eventually stapled inside of paper castles the children made and decorated. As a class, we discussed the essential elements of a complete story. Then, we brainstormed various beginnings, middles, and endings that made sense with our castle theme. The students were allowed to collaborate with their partners as they were planning their stories. My mentor, my supervisor, and I helped students organize their ideas and kept them on task. However, most of the children wrote their stories independently.

When I compared the stories from the last workshop to the stories from the first workshop, I was pleased to see that 15 of the 17 students that were present for the last workshop were able to meet the district benchmark for writing. When I checked the final scores of the 11 children who did not meet the benchmark during the first workshop, I noticed that 8 of them were able to meet the benchmark. Two children did not meet the benchmark because their stories lacked effective endings. One child did not participate in the final writing activity because he was absent on that day. The students who were meeting the district's benchmark when I began my project continued to experience success. In fact, as the workshops progressed, 2 children raised their scores above the benchmark by incorporating dazzling language and engaging plots in their work.

After examining the students' work throughout my workshops, I can claim that the minilessons and writing activities that I developed were effective for many struggling writers. Several students linger at the borderline. They are not yet consistent in their abilities to create complete stories independently. However, many children did experience remarkable growth in only six lessons, and they made important progress toward meeting their writing goals for second grade.

Setting Expectations

Inappropriate expectations discouraged many of the learners in my classroom and hindered my effectiveness as a writing teacher.

During my initial planning for my project, I was overflowing with ideas. After several years of imagining my own approach to writing instruction, I had an opportunity to actually implement some of my own lessons. I collected children's literature, planned discussion questions, made charts for brainstorming, and developed rubrics. I pushed the students to write entire stories during one session. I was incredibly enthusiastic and I got carried away.

By my second workshop, I was feeling quite discouraged. I was trying to generate excitement and creativity, and even my most capable writers were starting to grumble and complain. The children became fidgety and distracted during the lengthy discussions. They resisted the writing activities. The rubrics that I provided were either ignored or filled in hastily and without much reflection. The stories were not improving and none of us seemed to be having fun.

The setting workshop was discouraging from the beginning. When I asked the students what they had learned in the previous workshop, they remembered that they "drew pictures of what [they] imagined in [their] minds" and discussed "picture painting words" (scripted notes, 2/21). However, I had to question them for several minutes before anyone mentioned characters, which had been the focus of the lesson. After this review, I did a read-aloud, we drew pictures, I led a discussion, we brainstormed some ideas, I read another story, and we brainstormed again. The lesson was lengthy and, to be honest, quite boring. At one point, a student asked, "Can we go back and write?" I continued with my failing lesson even though the children were clearly telling me that my efforts were not helping them.

My frustration was evident in my journal entry. As I reflected on the setting workshop, I wrote, "I think I tried to pile too much into the morning. Their attention just could not last through all of the activities I had planned. I think my problems teaching really showed up in the children's writing, because only a few of them really described their settings in their stories." When my lessons were not developmentally appropriate, my students could sense my frustration and they got the message that writing was boring and confusing. For the first time, I began to realize that my personal experiences with writing as a young child were challenges rather than assets for me as a writing teacher. I always enjoyed writing and, in elementary school, I sought out extra opportunities to put my thoughts on paper. This passion for writing has certainly enriched my life, but it creates difficulties when I am attempting to relate to a student who does not share my enthusiasm. At the beginning of my project, I truly struggled to approach writing with a second graders' needs and abilities in mind, and my students responded to my first few lessons with boredom and confusion.

My students were my most valuable resource as I created developmentally appropriate expectations.

As I discussed my plans and my concerns with Linda (my mentor) and Nancy (my supervisor), I began to realize that I was not truly giving the students a fair chance to practice each story part because they had to write an entire story after each lesson.

Therefore, we decided to break apart our next story and write it one piece at a time. This change would lighten the workload, shorten the work time, and give us more time to practice and reflect on each story element. As I planned, I kept thinking about the student who groaned, "Do we have to write a whole story *again?*" Above all, I wanted my students to enjoy writing and feel successful as writers. Therefore, I needed to pay attention when they gave me warnings that they were feeling frustrated and overwhelmed.

When I shortened the minilessons and made my writing expectations more appropriate for second graders, I felt much more effective as a writing teacher because I was giving my students (and myself) a chance to feel successful. I noticed that the students were more attentive during the lessons and they were more willing to write. I did not hear any grumbling or complaining about writing one section of a story, and several students actually wanted more time than I gave them to write.

I understand writing as a writer, but I do not understand it as well from a writing teacher's perspective. As I continue to meet and work with new students, I must develop strategies for deciding what types of expectations are developmentally appropriate for them as writers. During my project, I quickly learned that "children can provide important data about their own learning" (Avery, 1993, p. 420). The students were sending me urgent messages with their grumbling, their body language, their writing, and their responses to me.

When I compared the students' presurveys to their postsurveys, I noticed a few patterns. During the presurvey, when the students were asked about their favorite kind of writing, many children mentioned writing activities such as Child of the Week, math journals, and science papers. As I read these responses, I was confronted with one of my biases. When I think of writing, I automatically think of stories. The students' responses reminded me that various genres of writing are integrated into every part of our day and these different kinds of writing experiences allow students with different strengths and needs to shine. As a teacher, I need to open my mind to the various styles of and purposes for writing so that I can engage all of my students in writing activities that give them opportunities to express their ideas and opinions.

When I read about the students' favorite and least favorite parts of writing on the postsurveys, I noticed that several students enjoyed "coming up with ideas," but "writing the words" was considered tedious and difficult. As I worked on this project, I began to realize that asking a young child to write a complete story is a daunting request. First, they must think of an idea and develop that idea until it has a beginning, a middle, and an end. Then, they must organize their thoughts and hold them in their minds long enough to get them on paper in sequence. These steps are quite difficult alone, but the task is more difficult for students who struggle with spelling, grammar, and letter formation. I am not surprised that children become frustrated when they have wonderful ideas and they have to endure the painstaking process of committing those ideas to paper. I was encouraged, however, when several children stated that they enjoyed developing ideas for their own original stories.

I found other evidence in the surveys that indicated that the writer's workshops helped some students become more confident about their writing ability. On his presurvey, one child wrote, "My least favorite part of writing is the ending because I do not like to solve the problem." When I interviewed this child, he told me that he struggled with endings and he thought that studying endings in our reading group was helpful. When I read his postsurvey, I was pleased to see that he wrote, "I like all of them the same because they are fun to do." On the postsurveys, some children were able to articulate their favorite parts of writing by using the language we used during our discussions. For example, one student wrote, "My favorite part of writing is the middles of stories because I like to make up adventures in my stories."

As a writer, I tend to be quite emotional about my work and I judge my writing based on the way I feel about it. I was fascinated when I realized that some children look at writing in a very quantitative way. When I asked them whether they were good writers, some children consistently relied on tangible evidence to support their answers. On his presurvey, a student wrote, "I think I am a good writer because I already have a published book." After the workshops were over, this student used a similar tool to measure his progress. He wrote, "I think I am a good writer because I am already working on my hardback," on his postsurvey. Other children used the scores on their stories to prove that they were good writers.

When I read one postsurvey, I became quite concerned. The student wrote that she was not a good writer because she "can't think of ideas." This response came from a child who often says that she "hates school." She resists assignments and, although she is extremely capable, she works slowly and her writing and coloring are sloppy. When I helped this student write the story that would be published in her hardback book, she would not put words down on paper unless I repeatedly prompted her. She told me her entire story, and then when I asked her what she wanted to write next, she said, "I don't know." This student is an excellent reader, and she can put wonderful language in her stories. However, her writing is often disorganized and difficult to understand. When I reviewed my comments from her portfolio and from the four stories she wrote during my writer's workshops, I consistently wrote that the parts of her stories did not relate and, therefore, her stories were not understandable and her endings did not solve the problem. I was not surprised that this student reacted negatively to writing because she has a similar reaction to most activities at school. However, I am concerned because she transferred her criticisms from the activity to herself. After she turned in her survey, I pulled her aside and told her about some aspects of her writing that I really enjoy. She just shrugged her shoulders and repeated, "I don't like it." The other students seem to either enjoy or accept writing. They are beginning to see themselves as part of a community of writers. I worry that this one student will be isolated from that community if I cannot find a way to motivate her as a writer.

Rubrics were helpful for some students, but they were not effective for other students.

When I created the rubrics for each of my lessons, I hoped that they would help the students organize their thoughts and remember the important ideas from my lessons. As I reflected on the writer's workshops in my journal, I wrote the following:

Although the children seem to understand the parts of stories during our discussions and they seem to try to apply them in their own writing, the rubrics do not seem to be very meaningful. The children do not refer to the rubrics during their writing unless I continually prompt them, and they often just race through it at the end of their writing as an afterthought. However, I still think they should be able to see the goals clearly before, during, and after writing if they are expected to meet those goals in their stories.

Nancy helped me take a more critical look at the rubrics I had created. I divided each story element into three parts. In each of the three sections, I included the main concept and then a few notes or questions that I considered prompts. I thought that these details would encourage the students' thinking, but they actually seemed to overwhelm the children and make them unsure of whether they had met each goal. I could tell that the rubrics were not helpful because I often found them left carelessly on the floor. During the third workshop, a student approached me with his rubric and asked, "What's this for?" My rubrics were not a useful resource for the children because the way that I thought about stories and the ways that they thought about stories were different. I needed to find a way to present the expectations for the story elements in a way that was meaningful for my second graders.

Then, while I was visiting my mother's first-grade classroom, she showed me a rubric that another first-grade class had created. The teacher listed scores from zero to six, and the children determined the characteristics of a story that would receive each score. The children had expressed their expectations in clear, simple terms. For example, a child who received a zero "did not write." These young writers knew that they were making decisions as they wrote and that those decisions had consequences for their writing. By asking students to articulate the decisions they make as they write, teachers are encouraging awareness. "Self-awareness leads to self-evaluation and, in turn, thoughtful decision making" (Avery, 1993, p. 417). I decided that my learners should be invited to be a part of setting the expectations that I was using to evaluate their stories. I hoped that, by being a part of creating the expectations, the students would feel more ownership and would begin to use the rubrics more thoughtfully.

During the fifth writer's workshop, my students and I focused on endings. After we discussed endings and the students wrote endings for their stories, I told the students that we were going to put together what we had learned about the different parts of stories. I said that the list they created during our discussion would be the checklist for their castle stories the next week. I took notes as the students suggested ideas, and I was amazed by how much information they had gathered about stories. As I recorded their ideas, I tried to use their words so that I would not add my influence to their expectations. When I created the checklist for the complete story workshop, I used the students' ideas. The expectations were expressed in clear, concise phrases. Hearing the students articulate their ideas helped me begin to understand the way an appropriate expectation for a second-grade writer should sound and look.

During the complete story workshop, I did not notice that the students used the checklists more or less than before. When I interviewed a small group of students, I invited them to compare a rubric that I wrote and the rubric that they wrote. I asked, "Did one of these checklists help you more, or were they both about the same?" One child replied, "The complete story checklist helped more because it helped you do a whole story in one day really quick." The students did not seem to care that they had written one rubric and I had written the other. I think that the students would have felt more ownership if they had been involved in creating the rubrics throughout the series of workshops. When I asked them to share their expectations for the last workshop, they basically reiterated the ideas I had emphasized during instruction. I am not surprised that they did not think of the checklist as their ideas.

During my interview, I also asked, "Do checklists help you write?" I could not tell simply by observing whether my rubrics had been effective for the students. One child replied, "Yes, because I could check down everything I did. Step by step." Another child agreed by saying, "I think it's good because the first thing I do is look at it and it says 'dazzling first sentence,' so I just think of one." Another student responded emphatically. She said, "No, because it makes you think, 'Oh, my story isn't very good, so I have to do better.'" She elaborated, "I like my stories how I like them. I don't like other people judging them just because they think they don't have any detail. I like it the way it is."

Once again, I was reminded of the wide range that characterizes second-grade writers. While one student found comfort in the opportunity to organize his thoughts, another student saw it as a threat to her as a writer. I began to realize that second-grade teachers need to develop ranges of strategies for teaching writing that are as varied as the unique writers in their rooms.

Collaboration

Collaborating with others helped some students develop ideas and grow as writers.

I was not sure what to expect when I assigned partners and allowed the students to brainstorm with their partners before writing. However, I was anxious to add this type of prewriting to my workshops. According to Calkins (1986), talking is a better form of prewriting for second graders than drawing because their ideas are becoming more detailed and complicated. As the students chat casually about their stories, they focus on content rather than the mechanics of putting their ideas down on paper. This takes the students' attention away from the "right way" to approach their writing and helps them realize that "they have something to say and a voice with which to say it" (p. 70).

I was amazed by the way that my role in the classroom changed when I allowed the students to support each other during writer's workshop. I usually found myself talking with one writer after another. As I traveled around the room, students who were struggling would begin to trail after me with their papers clutched in their hands. I was putting all of my effort into keeping the students' pencils moving, so I didn't have time to have a meaningful discussion with a student who was struggling with writer's block or a complicated idea. When the students brainstormed with their partners, I found that my role was less frantic. I could talk quietly with a student who was concerned about his or her writing. I could eavesdrop on conversations to gain insight into the students' thinking. The students were becoming a community of writers, and they were beginning to realize that the teachers were not the only people in the room who could help them when they encountered problems in their writing.

These partnerships seemed to be the most helpful for students with average writing ability. I enjoyed participating in their conversations and I saw wonderfully creative ideas emerge as the children worked together. When a group of two boys met, they realized that one partner wrote a beginning about a dragon and the other partner wrote a beginning about a knight. They began discussing potential problems for their stories. When I visited their conference, they proudly told me that they were going to use the same problem for their stories. One writer described the problem from the dragon's perspective and the other writer described the problem from the knight's perspective. Another writer was struggling to start his castle story and his partner suggested some ideas that helped him begin. He acknowledged her help by naming the heroine of his story after her.

Other students found that collaborating with others was ineffective for them as writers.

I found that the student partnerships were not very effective for the special needs students in our room and for the most independent, fluent writers in our room. The students who were struggling as writers needed a great deal of support from teachers as they were developing their ideas and as they were putting their ideas on paper. They rarely had time to give each other feedback because they were putting all of their energy into creating their own stories.

The most fluent, independent writers in the classroom were partners during the workshops. During the interview, when I asked about working with partners, Kate replied, "It's fun, but we just have our own ideas. Charlie says something and it kind of gives me an idea, but it doesn't go well with my story. So, then I do another idea. Then, I ask Charlie if he wants to do this idea, but he changes it around, so it gets confusing." When I reviewed my supervisor's notes from watching this team's peer conference, I noticed that they did not really interact. They stated their ideas out loud, but they seemed to ignore each other. These students had their ideas in place, and they did not seem open to considering other ideas.

Finally, during the interview, another student told me that he did not enjoy working with his partner. When I asked him to elaborate, he said, "He always had to go away from me." During several workshops, we had behavior problems with this student's partner. The boys were often separated, so the partnership was not helpful for them.

Connections to Literature

Students who make connections between writing and reading can use literature to help them solve problems when they are writing.

Routman states that, as teachers, "we must immerse our students in outstanding literature every day" to "help them notice how the author has dealt with the topic, genre, organization, setting, mood, word choice, sentence construction, and more" (p. 221). Throughout this project, I was amazed by the ways that the students used the literature around them to solve problems in their own writing. When they had difficulty finding ideas, several students turned to literature for inspiration.

Dana wrote a story called "The Knights and the Dragon" shortly after we read *The Paperbag Princess* by Robert Munsch. In her story, Dana's knights defeated a dragon with clever tricks that resembled the tricks Elizabeth used in *The Paperbag Princess*:

> Then the knights came out and said is it trew [*sic*] that you can drink 30 gallons of water in only 5 seconds? The dragon said yes so he did. Then the knight said can you fly and stay up for three whole days? The dragon said yes so he did. All those three days he was still up. The dragon was egsasted [*sic*] on the third day.

In her previous story, Dana had difficulty writing an ending that solved her problem. By using Munsch as a model, she tackled this problem and was able to bring her story to a satisfying end.

When I read Jack's story, I noticed that he was making connections between writing at school and reading at home. His story, "It All Started Out from an Egg," echoes J. K. Rowling's *Harry Potter and the Sorcerer's Stone*:

> Ocne [*sic*] there was a wizared [*sic*] named Hegred. Hegred found an egg it was relly [*sic*] big so he figrd [*sic*] that it was a dragon's egg. So he took it back to his cottage in the woods and put it over his fire to keep it warm. In 15 days it hatched it was a boy dragon in five day [*sic*] he was bigger than hegred [*sic*] and sarted [*sic*] to nock [*sic*] out the walls and started to blow fire and burning [*sic*] Hegred's house down.

Jack also wrote a retelling of *Cinderella* during another writer's workshop. He has wonderful ideas and excellent language, but he seems to be more comfortable writing when he begins in a familiar place. He raises hermit crabs with his brother and sister, and he often uses the hermit crabs as characters in his stories. By starting with familiar ideas, Jack has gained the confidence to take risks by using more descriptive language and reading his stories to his classmates.

During my inquiry project, my reading group was reading a version of *The Ugly Duckling*. Charlie, a student in my reading group, mentioned his dissatisfaction with the story's message during several group discussions. In *The Ugly Dragon*, Charlie used his voice as a writer to approach issues that made him uncomfortable as a reader:

Once upon a time in an enchanted forest with surprizes [*sic*] anywhere you went there lurked a kind and friendly dragon. It was raining cats and dogs. She laied [*sic*] 30 eggs. Every egg was silver except one. It was gold. One day when the sun was boiling like an oven the eggs hatched. One after another. All of them looked like the mommy dragon except one. The one had gold scaly skin and cotton white teeth and the eyes were root beer brown. It was very good looking when the sun was shining on its back. All of the other dragons teased him. The one dragon was sweet and kind while the others were mean and furious and greedy.

During reading group discussions, Charlie used the illustrations in *The Ugly Duckling* to argue that the main character was different, not ugly. When I read *The Ugly Dragon*, I noticed that Charlie immediately established that his main character "was very good looking when the sun was shining on its back." Charlie also revised the end of the well-known tale. His ugly dragon met and befriended a giant without having to change his appearance at all. I was surprised and pleased when I noticed that Charlie was connecting reading experiences that happened outside of our workshops with his writing. He was truly reading as a writer, and his writing incorporated the insights that he gained as a reader.

Students who are immersed in quality literature incorporate more literary language in their writing.

For me, writing is exciting and empowering because it gives me a chance to put my voice on paper. "Voice is hard to define, but when it's in—or missing from—a piece of writing, you sense it. Writing with voice has richness and sparkle, a distinct human spirit that makes you feel you know the writer" (Routman, 2002, p. 222). Throughout the series of writer's workshops, I approached the issue of voice with my students by focusing on "dazzling" language. We searched for dazzling words as we read children's literature, we brainstormed dazzling words as we prepared to write, and we celebrated dazzling words in our peers' stories. I used literature and the checklists to encourage the children to use "dazzling first sentences" in their beginnings, "dazzling action words" in their middles, and "dazzling feeling words" in their endings. I also incorporated the search for dazzling words into my reading group instruction. As they read, the children recorded descriptive language. Then, they chose an interesting word or phrase and studied it more carefully by completing a word web.

The students responded eagerly to this aspect of the writer's workshops. Anna Quindlen's description of her heroine in *Happily Ever After* included the phrase "her eyes were the color of root beer." After I read this description to my students, I found similar phrases in at least five stories. I also noticed that the "dazzling language" appeared in stories written by students with a variety of writing abilities. This aspect of writing seemed to appeal to many of the children, and they wanted their readers to be impressed with their word choices:

> "Ok said Mini in her tinest vos [*sic*]"; "One snowy cold day when the snow was falling like little cotten [*sic*] balls deep down in the forist [*sic*] there was a princess named Sofy. Her hair was the color of the sun and her eyes were the color of the sky, and her skin was the most peachiest peach you ever did see"; ". . , that nasty fox came prowling along . . ."; and "Then the room groo [*sic*] silent."

As I compared the students' stories throughout the workshops, I also noticed that their language was becoming more literary. During the first workshop, Henry tried to include the descriptive language that was discussed during the minilesson. He has many details, but his sentences sound more like a list than a story:

> "His name was Charlie. Charlie was a boy [*sic*] he was 26 years old and had a little brother named Cameron. Charlie has brown hair and his brother has blond hair."

During the last writer's workshop, Henry wrote a story in which the descriptive language flows more naturally:

> One cold winter day in January there was a feirs dragon named Jack who had an advencher with a knight named Sam. Jack never let a sigal soul past him. Jack liked to

practice roring and he liked to go into the casal and burn things like bowlse and pots.

As my students' voices began to emerge in their stories, I noticed a growing enthusiasm for sharing stories with others. When volunteers read their work aloud to the class, the students always made comments about the dazzling language.

Students who read from a writer's perspective are comfortable thinking critically about literature.

Writing can be an extremely intimidating task. Many children approach published literature as "polite guests" because they get the implicit message that printed words cannot be challenged (Calkins, 1986, p. 223). As a writing teacher, I wanted to be very careful about the message that I sent to my students as I shared literature. I hoped that my students would learn to think critically about every text they read, rather than viewing published books as "final and unquestionable" (Calkins, p. 224). Therefore, during the minilessons, I encouraged the students to respond to the literature with both praise and criticism.

Throughout the series of minilessons, I noticed that the students' comments were becoming more and more sophisticated. They were thinking about the choices that the authors made, and they were becoming more comfortable sharing their opinions about the effectiveness of the authors' writing. Their comments became more thoughtful during literature discussions, student sharings, and reading groups:

When people start to read it, they don't want to stop.

I would recommend this book to others because it teaches you a lesson. Don't be mean to others just because they are different.

He didn't name the characters. He just called them prince and princess. I think it would be good if they had names.

I'd say he needs to work more on the descriptive action words.

I would not recommend this story to another reader because the author didn't put a lot of detail at the end.

I think it's good because it's like a mystery. You want to see what happens next. (Scripted notes, 3/14)

During the final writer's workshop, I realized that my students had become quite comfortable thinking critically about published literature. I wanted to practice using the "Complete Story Checklist" with the whole group, so I read *Cabbage Rose* by M. C. Helldorfer and we completed the checklist as a class. I assumed that, because *Cabbage Rose* was a published book, the students would think it was well written. As our discussion progressed, I noticed that the children were suggesting that the author needed to keep working on many aspects of the book. They also disagreed with each other's opinions about the story:

Sarah: I think we should give it a check because there was no adventure in it.

David: I think it's a star because she went on an adventure to the castle. (Scripted notes, 3/21)

The thoughtfulness of their comments and the confidence with which those comments were delivered showed me that my students were becoming more critical thinkers.

The students in Room 20 are members of a writing community that includes published authors.

Calkins (1986) describes reading as a chance for young writers to "learn from their more skillful colleagues" (p. 221). As my project progressed, I was encouraged by evidence that suggested that my students were thinking of themselves as writers. During one morning greeting, I asked the students to share a favorite fairy tale character. I was amazed and pleased when several of them asked if they could name characters from their own writing. They were placing their writing in the same category as the books they were reading, and published authors were their equals rather than their superiors. For me as a writer and a writing teacher, this is the most satisfying outcome. If my students leave second grade knowing that they are writers, I will feel that I have succeeded as a writing teacher. (Russell, 2002)

In addition to noting the ways Julie built a case for each of her 10 claims through stringing together pieces of evidence from multiple data sources to support her learning, there are two additional noteworthy points to highlight from the main text of Julie's inquiry write-up that appears on the previous pages.

First, notice under Claim 3 that when Julie discusses patterns from her survey, she ends by discussing one child that did not fit into any of the patterns she previously mentions:

> . . . When I read one postsurvey, I became quite concerned. The student wrote that she was not a good writer because she "can't think of ideas." This response came from a child who often says that she "hates school." She resists assignments and, although she is extremely capable, she works slowly. . . . I am not surprised that this student reacted negatively to writing because she has a similar reaction to most activities at school. . . . However, I am concerned because she transferred her criticisms from the activity to herself. . . . The other students seem to either enjoy or accept writing. They are beginning to see themselves as part of a community of writers. I worry that this one student will be isolated from that community if I cannot find a way to motivate her as a writer.

While teacher-inquirers are often quite excited about finding patterns in their data and are most apt to report those patterns when writing, it is also insightful to look at data that do not fit and also include explanations in the write-up of an inquiry of why those data do not fit. Research methodologists commonly refer to this as "negative cases." It is often through looking critically at data that do not fit and reporting this in your writing that you learn more about the patterns themselves. In addition, reporting about data that do not fit enhances the credibility of your inquiry. In the absence of sharing negative data, you risk painting an unrealistic portrait of your classroom that can be met with skepticism by your audience who know well that nothing that occurs within the vast complexities of teaching is simple. Reporting your negative data contributes to creating a picture of your learning that rings true to life.

Second, note that each of Julie's 10 claims was supported by multiple sources of data, but not nearly all the data Julie had collected over the two months of her inquiry, or that she had sorted into categories during data analysis. Through her writing, Julie selected the most powerful pieces of data to represent the patterns she found and the statements of her learning. Realize that as you construct your case to support statements of your learning through inquiry, you may experience difficulty selecting which data excerpts to use. As Wolcott (1990) notes:

> The major problem we face . . . is not to get data, but to get rid of it! With writing comes the always painful task (at least from the standpoint of the person who gathered it) of winnowing material to a manageable length, communicating only the essence rather than exhibiting the bulky catalogues that testify to one's painstaking thoroughness. (p. 18)

Once the winnowing down is completed and your arguments clearly articulated, the last step in writing up your inquiry is providing conclusions.

Step 4: Providing Concluding Thoughts

When you read a good mystery, you expect that the conclusion of the book will provide answers to solve the mystery. Similarly, as you near the end of writing up your work to share it, you may conceive of concluding thoughts as being answers to the initial questions posed by the inquiry study. Sometimes, this might be the case. However, just as often, concluding thoughts do not answer the initial research question, but generate additional questions and further areas for inquiry.

Recall in Chapter 5, where we discussed data analysis, we shared that the work of a teacher-researcher is never quite finished as good data analyses generate more questions than answers. It is difficult to conceive of how to finish a piece of writing when the work of a teacher-researcher is never done. Many teacher-inquirers finish their work by reflecting in general on the specific inquiry just completed, generating directions for the future and stating further wonderings. We end this chapter with the concluding passage from Julie's paper. As you read, note how she used these three techniques to bring closure to her written work.

The Next Step

During my last writer's workshop, as Linda was walking around the room, she paused at Michael's desk. Michael faces many obstacles in the classroom, and writing is particularly challenging. At the beginning of the year, we struggled to get him to pick up his pencil at all. Linda began to read over Michael's shoulder, and then she asked the whole class to stop working and listen to the beginning of Michael's new story:

> One morning when the sun was makeing [*sic*] it's way over the montons [*sic*] to shine so the erth [*sic*] has some lite [*sic*]. A batel [*sic*] was going to begin. On a lowd speeker [*sic*] a king said knights begin the batel [*sic*]. The knights started smacking sords [*sic*] to gether [*sic*] and it sonded [*sic*] like thunder.

The other students complimented him enthusiastically, and he began to beam. Linda encouraged him to work hard and finish the story, and he was able to score above the benchmark for second grade.

When I heard Linda read those words, and I saw the way the other children supported Michael's efforts, I got tears in my eyes. For me, this project was filled with these magical, dazzling moments. I found that teaching writing is filled with challenges. I also found that confronting those challenges and pushing myself as a teacher make writing instruction even more engaging and exciting than I had hoped it would be. I learned that every student in my room has something dazzling to say, and my job is to help him or her find his or her voice.

Finally, I learned that my journey as a writing teacher is just beginning. I was not able to help my second graders grow as writers until I began thinking about writing from their perspective and tailoring my instruction toward them and their needs. Therefore, my workshops will change with each group of young writers that enters my classroom. After doing this project, I am able to see that challenge as a wonderful chance to grow as a teacher.

As I completed my project, many wonderings remained. One huge challenge for the future is finding a way to give young writers "the luxury of time" (Calkins, 1986, p. 23). During the interview, I asked the children to tell me how I could help them grow as writers. I was surprised when one student said, ". . . maybe you could let us be." She wanted uninterrupted time to put her thoughts on paper. I agree that students need time to just write if they are going to develop a love for writing. However, after this year, I realize that finding this time will be an enormous task. Managing time is difficult for me, but I cannot ignore this crucial part of writing instruction. As I develop a schedule next year, I will need to continue to listen to my students as I establish priorities and make decisions.

Routman encourages teachers to "take the risk of writing in front of [their] students" (2002, p. 211). I wanted to incorporate this element into my workshops, but I was not brave enough to show my writing to my students. I felt enormous tension because I was asking my students to do something that I was not willing to do myself. Next year, my first challenge as a writing teacher will be sharing my own writing with my students. I am nervous, but I am also curious about the effect my writing might have upon the workshop environment. I was incredibly impressed by the writing community that my students created this year, and I would be honored to be an active part of that community. (Russell, 2002)

Exercises

1. Outline an inquiry write-up for your study using the four components of a write-up shared in this chapter: (1) providing background information, (2) sharing the design of the inquiry (procedures, data collection, and data analysis), (3) stating the learning and supporting the statements with data, and (4) providing concluding thoughts.

2. Write one component at a time, sharing drafts of completed components with a colleague, your mentor, your intern, a university supervisor, or a family member to serve as a critical friend to offer feedback on your writing.

The End of Your   7
Journey: Making
Your Inquiry Public

Back in Chapter 2, you began your inquiry journey by finding and defining your first wondering. Since then, you have navigated different components of the inquiry process—collaboration, data collection, data analysis, and writing up your work. You are nearing the end of your journey, but there are still a few last steps that must be taken to make your journey complete. These last steps involve making your inquiry public through the sharing of your work with others.

WHY IS IT IMPORTANT TO
SHARE MY WORK WITH OTHERS?

To illustrate the importance of sharing your work with others, imagine that as you start the last leg of your journey, you notice a large pond that is stagnant and you are enticed to create some type of movement or change in the water. As you near the edge, you notice that numerous large stones surround the pond. You reach down, pick up a stone, and toss it as far out into the center of the pond as your strength allows you. Lying beside the pond, the stone had no chance of impacting the water. But once tossed in, the stone not only disturbs the stillness of the water in the immediate vicinity of where it landed but also creates ripples of water that emanate out from the stone's landing place and that eventually reach the perimeter of the pond.

An unshared teacher inquiry is like the stone lying beside the pond. Unless that inquiry is tossed into the professional conversation and dialog that contributes to the knowledge base for teaching, the inquiry has little chance of creating change. However, once tossed in, the inquiry disturbs the status quo of educational practices, creating a ripple effect, beginning with the teacher himself or herself and his or her immediate vicinity (the students and his or her classroom) and emanating out to a school, a district, a state, eventually reaching and contributing to the transformation of the perimeter of all practice—the profession of teaching itself.

Hence, it is critical that you "get into the pond" and share your inquiry for yourself, for your students, for other teachers, and for the profession. For you, the process of preparing your findings to share with others helps you to clarify your own thinking about your work. In addition to clarifying your own thinking, in the actual sharing of your work, you give other professionals access to your thinking so that they can question, discuss, debate, and relate. This process helps you and your colleagues push and extend your thinking about practice as well.

Clarifying, pushing, and extending thinking are not the only benefits of sharing for you and your colleagues. Fellow professionals also benefit from the knowledge you created. For example, veteran teacher researcher George Dempsie's passion for utilizing puppets as a form of pedagogy with young children led him to study and publish the results of this practice (Dempsie, 1997, 2000). In his own district, he has inspired puppetry as pedagogy in dozens of teachers, across 11 different elementary buildings. In addition, as a mentor-teacher in a professional development school, sharing his research with interns has inspired a large percentage of these new teachers to use puppets as a way to gain access into children's thinking. His presentations at conferences and publications allow his work to spread outside his immediate vicinity (classroom, school, and district) as well.

For your students, sharing your inquiry with other professionals can change the very ways these children experience schooling. For example, we know one student-teacher who completed an inquiry on a second-grade child who was having great difficulty fitting into the structure of schooling, but was not receiving any services because she did not qualify in traditional ways. Her inquiry illuminated many critical insights into the child that traditional forms of assessment would not have generated. Becoming an advocate for this child, the student-teacher and her cooperating teacher shared the results of her inquiry with other specialists and the principal. Eventually, a full-time paraprofessional was hired to work individually with this child within the regular classroom each school day. In a year's time, the child made great strides forward in her academic and social development.

We have provided just two specific examples here to illustrate the power, and therefore, necessity of sharing inquiry. Some inquiries inspire small, local change. Some inspire large, sweeping change. All change, large or small, is significant in that the changes that are occurring are emanating from those best positioned to make a difference in education, and those that for years have been kept from making that difference— teachers themselves!

Kincheloe (1991) writes about the ways teachers have been kept from making that difference using a comparison between teachers and peasants within a Third World culture with hierarchical power structures, scarce resources, and traditional values:

> Like their third world counterparts, teachers are preoccupied with daily survival—time for reflection and analysis seems remote and even quite fatuous given the crisis management atmosphere and the immediate attention survival necessitates. In such a climate those who would suggest that more time and resources be delegated to reflective and growth-inducing pursuits are viewed as impractical visionaries devoid of common sense. Thus, the status quo is perpetuated, the endless cycle of underdevelopment rolls on with its peasant culture of low morale and teachers as "reactors" to daily emergencies. (p. 12)

By getting into the pond and sharing your inquiry, as a teacher, you contribute to breaking the cycle described above. You contribute to educational reform: "The plethora of small changes made by critical teacher researchers around the world in individual classrooms may bring about far more authentic educational reform than the grandiose policies formulated in state or national capitals" (Kincheloe, 1991, p. 14).

By getting into the pond and sharing your inquiry, you contribute to changing the ways some people outside of teaching view teachers and their practice and try to change education from the outside in. In the sharing of your inquiry, you contribute to reforming the profession of teaching—from the inside out!

WHAT ARE SOME WAYS
I MIGHT SHARE MY WORK?

There are many structures in place that offer you opportunities to share your teacher inquiry. If you have written up your work, you have not only clarified your thinking, but you have produced a product that can easily be shared with others in multiple ways. First, you might begin simply by sharing your written work with local colleagues, your principal, or other professionals, asking them for some feedback. This sharing could potentially lead to the formation of a study group to discuss your particular inquiry and related topics. Another way to share your written work is to submit it to one of the many journals designed with a teacher-researcher audience in mind such as *Teacher Research: The Journal of Classroom Inquiry* and *Teaching and Learning: The Journal of Naturalistic Inquiry*. Finally, you can share your written work on-line by exploring one of the many action research Web sites, listservs, and on-line journals. Teacher inquiries completed by prospective and practicing teachers within the professional development schools where we have worked are available at http://www.ed.psu.edu/pds. Other action research Web sites and journals summarized by Mills (2003) include *Educational Action Research* at http://www.triangle.co.uk/ear-o.htm, *Networks* at http://www.oise.utoronto.ca/-ctd/networks/, *Action Research International* at http://www.scu.edu.au/schools/gcm/ar/ari/arihome.html, *Action Research Electronic Reader* at http://www.cchs.usyd.edu.au/arow/rader/index.htm welcome.htm, *Participatory Action Research Network (PARnet)* at http://www.parnet.org, *The Collaborative Action Research Network* at www.uea. ac.uk/care/carn, and *Centre for Action Research in Professional Practice (CARPP)* at www.bath.ac.uk/carpp. We hope you will explore some of these excellent on-line outlets for your written work.

If you were not sold on writing in Chapter 6, we believe there are other mechanisms that give the learning that occurs from an inquiry a form so that it can be shared. These alternative mechanisms also engage teacher-inquirers in the process of clarifying thinking in a fashion similar to writing. We have witnessed the creation of posters, iMovies, and Powerpoint presentations as powerful ways to share an inquiry that either complement or take the place of producing a formal write-up.

Many teacher-inquirers use these mechanisms to share their work orally in informal and more formal ways. Informally, some groups of teacher-inquirers organize a gathering outside of the school structure (e.g., an after-school meeting at a coffee shop) to discuss their work. Or, if you are enrolled in an undergraduate or graduate class in which teacher inquiry is a focus, you may culminate the semester with a special meeting (perhaps a potluck dinner) where all share the results of their inquiry endeavors.

Within the school structure, formal sharing by teacher-inquirers is often accomplished through dedicating special portions of faculty meetings to inquiry or totally reconceptualizing faculty meetings to allow space for the ongoing sharing of inquiry (Dana, 1994, 1995). Some districts also devote entire inservice days to teacher inquiry, where colleagues gather to share their work. If you are not currently in a context where within-school structures for the sharing of inquiry like those described above are in place, you may begin the building of these structures simply by offering to talk for a few minutes about your work at a faculty meeting. Much of our own research has focused on building an inquiry culture (see, e.g., Dana, 1994, 1995, 2001; Dana & Silva, 2001, 2002; Silva & Dana, 1999). As a result of our research, we have learned that building a culture of inquiry takes time, and is best started slowly, as some of your current administrators and colleagues (if you are a veteran teacher) or future administrators and colleagues (if you are a prospective teacher) may be reluctant to embrace inquiry and the changes it necessitates. While building an inquiry culture is a slow process, it has to start somewhere, and it can start with you. Be patient, and persevere!

Finally, many teacher researchers present their work at conferences. There are numerous national forums that showcase presentations by teacher-inquirers. Perhaps the largest and most well known is the American Educational Research Association (AERA). The professionals who engage in teacher inquiry who are members of this organization assemble in a Special Interest Group called "Teachers as Researchers."

While we encourage you to become part of a national network such as AERA, the reality in almost every school district is that conference travel money for teachers is small or nonexistent. Many teachers receive limited support for conference endeavors and must pay out of their own pockets to attend and present. For this reason, the cost of national travel is often prohibitive for many teachers, especially on a yearly basis.

You can still experience the exhilaration that comes from presenting your work formally to an audience by connecting to conferences that occur in your vicinity. Most national organizations such as AERA described above and ASCD (Association for Supervision and Curriculum Development), NCTM (National Council for Teachers of Mathematics), NCSS (National Council for the Social Studies), NSTA (National Science Teachers Association), NCTE (National Council for Teachers of English), and ATE (Association of Teacher Educators) have state affiliates that hold conferences at least once a year. In addition, if you are a prospective teacher, most of these organizations offer very reasonable membership rates for students, so it is an excellent time to investigate professional groups that can serve as local outlets for the sharing of your inquiry, as well as a stimulus for continuing to inquire into your practice throughout your career. Finally, in addition to the journals dedicated solely to action research described previously, many of these state affiliate organizations also publish journals that offer another outlet for your written work (see, e.g., Dana, Gimbert, & Silva, 1999).

A final possibility for conferences is designing and holding your own teacher inquiry conference. While this may sound like an overwhelming undertaking, it can be accomplished relatively easily by starting small and drawing on some sound organizational abilities. To show the range and variety that is possible, we describe two structures we have used to create our own conferences. The first structure uses posters and is conversational. The second structure uses presented papers and follows a more traditional conference format.

The first structure was designed as a culmination to a class on teacher inquiry with just 13 members in the class. We held the final class on an evening in the all-purpose room of a local school (7:00 p.m.–9:00 p.m.), where class members set up posters that captured the essence of their inquiries in two different shifts (7:00–7:30 p.m. and 8:00–8:30 p.m.). Each member of the class was responsible for inviting at least one other colleague or family member, and we also posted information about the conference in local schools and at the university. We created a program for the evening that contained the titles and abstracts of each class member's work, and the schedule for the evening conference was as follows:

> 7:00–7:30 Round One of Poster Presentations (six posters set up)— Conference participants visit each poster and presenter discusses their inquiry and answers questions through conversation.

> 7:30–8:00 Refreshments served; Round One posters taken down; Round Two posters set up.

> 8:00–8:30 Round Two of Poster Presentations (seven posters set up)—Conference participants visit each poster and presenters discusses their inquiries and answer questions through conversation.

> 8:30–9:00 Participants gather for discussion and reflection about teacher inquiry.

The second structure was designed as a culmination to a professional development school year where mentors and interns shared the results of inquiries conducted in their classrooms that year (Dana, 1999). We designated the last Saturday in April as the annual Professional Development School Teacher Inquiry Conference. Two weeks prior to this conference, we asked all mentors and interns who had engaged in inquiry to e-mail us titles and brief abstracts of their work. We assigned each of the inquiry abstracts received to one of five 20-minute sessions that would occur concurrently throughout the morning in different neighboring classrooms at one of the professional development school sites. We invited teachers, administrators, faculty from the school district and university, as well as the family members of all presenters. Next, we created a conference program to allow all of the participants to view the presentation offerings and choose which sessions they wished to attend. After three concurrent

Figure 7.1 Inquiry Poster

sessions, we allotted a 30-minute time slot to refreshments we called "bagel brunch," offering coffee, juice, doughnuts, and, of course, bagels. After two more sessions, the conference ended just after the noon hour with recognition of all the presenters and those who supported their work and brief reflections on the inquiry process. One portion from the 2002 conference appears in Figure 7.2.

Remember our advice about starting small? The first conference program we organized during the pilot year of the PDS in 1999 contained a total of 13 intern presentations and one mentor-teacher presentation from two elementary professional development school sites. There were two or three selections to choose to attend during each concurrent session, and approximately 50 people attended the conference. Just four years later, this same conference had grown to showcase the inquiries of 41 interns, 15 mentor-teachers, 6 teachers who were not currently mentoring an intern, and 4 librarians from 6 elementary schools, 2 middle schools and the district's high school. Approximately 200 attendees chose from 10 or 11 presentations during each concurrent session. (For more information about building an inquiry culture, please see Dana, Silva, Gimbert, Nolan, Zembal-Saul, Tzur, Mule, & Sanders, 2001; Dana, Silva & Snow-Gerono, 2002; and Snow, Dana, & Silva, 2001).

Figure 7.2   Inquiry Conference Program

The State College Area School District—Pennsylvania State University Professional Development School Teacher Inquiry Conference
April 27, 2002
Mt. Nittany Middle School

9:00 a.m.   **Welcome and Orientation**
Auditorium

9:15–9:35 a.m.   **Session I**

Room 156 Encouraging Lifelong Learners: Intrinsic Motivation in the Classroom

Melissa Cinquini, Intern
Park Forest Elementary School
cinquini@psu.edu

How can we encourage students to become lifelong learners? This inquiry began with an assessment of students' current motivational responses to completing school work. The teacher then used these responses to explore how an activity rooted in guiding and supporting intrinsic motivation affected the learners in this classroom.

Room 154 Phonemic Awareness: A Key to Kindergarten

Darcie Hampton, Mentor
Matternville Elementary School
drh13@scasd.pa.k12.us

Beth Schickel, Intern
Matternville Elementary School
schickel@psu.edu

A veteran teacher and intern look at the learning and teaching of phonemic awareness. As teachers in a kindergarten classroom we noticed that students' sense of phonemic awareness varied a great deal. As a result of this, we wanted to see the effects of supplemental phonemic awareness activities with students who are struggling.

Room 152 Effective Use of the Opening Routine

Sara Evensen Tilles, Intern
Ferguson Township Elementary School
set132@psu.edu

A Professional Development School intern examines the use of various strategies during opening activities. How can all subject areas be integrated and reinforced during this time? How can students be motivated to participate?

Room 146 Developing Differentiated Instruction Strategies and Motivational Strategies to Meet the Individual Needs of a Math Learner

Stacee Banko, Intern
Park Forest Elementary School
smb295@psu.edu

I believe that it is crucial that students are motivated and excited to learn in every situation. This means that I must be willing to look at my own teaching styles and see where new strategies can be implemented as well as encouraged. My inquiry project focuses on an individual learner who was "slipping between the cracks" before I understood the different teaching strategies I could adopt to help him become a successful, motivated learner.

The growth of this conference attests to the power teacher inquiry holds for teacher professional growth, and brings us full circle to where we began this book. In the preface to this text we stated that "we hope to provide insights into the power teacher inquiry holds to transform classrooms and schools to places where knowledge about teaching and learning is generated from and used by those closest to the children—classroom teachers." We hope that as you end this text, you have enjoyed your journey through the basic tenets of the inquiry process, the ultimate

Figure 7.2   Continued

Room 144   Examining Different Types of Assessment and Evaluating Which Assessment Students Value the Most

Jamie Clouse, Intern
High School North
twirlygirl183@aol.com

There are numerous approaches to assessment, but it is crucial to choose the best type of assessment based on the assignment. Too often students believe that the only real way to measure their success is with a letter grade. I would like to explore various types of assessment to get a firmer grasp on which types of assessment are most supportive of a learning environment.

Room 256   Building Confidence in Reading

Jackie Mintmier, Intern
Ferguson Township Elementary School
jxm530@psu.edu

Through research and exploring two students' beliefs and thinking about reading, I tried to find ways that would help to increase the students' confidence and help them develop a positive self-image of themselves as readers.

Room 254   Effective Parent Communication: What Does it Look Like?

Candy Bryan, Teacher
Ferguson Township Elementary School
cjh14@scasd.k12.pa.us

Kelly Reilley-Kaminiski, Mentor
Ferguson Township Elementary School
kar15@scasd.k12.pa.us

Two elementary school teachers research effective parent communication tools that reflect the current needs within each classroom. Based on parent feedback, they implemented changes to their practices and compared the needs of the parents between first and third year students

Room 252   The Puzzle of Two Children: How to Motivate Two New and Challenging Students in My Classroom

Kelli Hollada, Intern
Radio Park Elementary School
keh164@psu.edu

In an attempt to discover how to best serve the students in my second grade class, I searched for ways to help motivate two boys who were experiencing difficulties as learners in my classroom.

Room 246   Responding to Conflict in a First-Grade Classroom

Meghan Marshall, Intern
Radio Park Elementary School
mlm335@psu.edu

An intern explores the conflicts in her first-grade classroom. What is causing our classroom, especially one group of girls, to have so much conflict? How can I better respond to these conflicts to encourage students to be independent problem solvers?

Room 244   Between a Rock and a Hard Place: The Search to Find a Meaningful and Practical Way to Assess Student Writing

Sabrina Ehmke, Intern
Mount Nittany Middle School
sae129@psu.edu

My inquiry involves the struggle I face as a teacher when it comes to evaluating student writing. The experience of writing, which seems to me inherently a subjective one, is more often than not assigned a point or grade value as an indicator of achievement. In the process of regulating writing to a quantitative variable, I wonder whether such a forced attempt at objectivity does in fact not only hinder students as writers, but also devalue what we as teachers hope to promote in terms of the act of writing itself.

Room 242   Mathematical Rubrics-Meeting the Standards

Brenda Khayat, Mentor
Park Forest Elementary
bgk11@scasd.k12.pa.us

My goal was to improve the written side of problem solving for fifth graders. The belief is that students can problem solve, but the challenge is for them to show it in their written explanations.

goal of which is *not* to produce an inquiry project, but to adopt a stance toward your teaching and the teaching profession that is characterized by continuous problematizing of practice, studying of practice, and leading change efforts based on the outcomes of such study. This is the ultimate journey on which we hope you will embark.

We believe no other author captures the nature of this ultimate journey as eloquently as William Ayers (1989) in the following quote we

Figure 7.3   Kelly Reilly-Kaminski and Candy Bryan Present Their Inquiry at the
Fourth Annual State College Area School District–Pennsylvania State
University Teacher Inquiry Conference

used at the very opening of this book. Coming full circle, we close our
book, as we began it:

> Teaching involves a search for meaning in the world. Teaching is
> a life project, a calling, a vocation that is an organizing center of
> all other activities. Teaching is past and future as well as present,
> it is background as well as foreground, it is depth as well as sur-
> face. Teaching is pain and humor, joy and anger, dreariness and
> epiphany. Teaching is world building, it is architecture and design,
> it is purpose and moral enterprise. Teaching is a way of being in
> the world that breaks through the boundaries of the traditional
> job and in the process redefines all life and teaching itself. (p. 130)

Through embarking on the inquiry journey, you break boundaries.
You redefine life. You redefine teaching itself . . . Bon voyage!

References

Acheson, K. A., & Gall, M. D. (1997). *Techniques in the clinical supervision of teachers: Preservice and inservice applications.* New York: Longman.

Almquist, C. (2000, April). *Science tables in first grade.* Paper presented at the second annual State College Area School District–Pennsylvania State University Teacher Inquiry Conference, State College, PA.

Aronowitz, S., & Giroux, H. (1985). *Education under seige.* New York: New World Foundation.

Avery, C. (1993). *. . . And with a light touch: Learning about reading, writing, and teaching with first graders.* Portsmouth, NH: Heinemann.

Ayers, W. (1989). *The good preschool teacher: Six teachers reflect on their lives.* New York: Teachers College Press.

Bigelow, B., & Peterson, B. (1998). *Rethinking Columbus: The next 500 years.* Milwaukee: Rethinking Schools LTD.

Borst, D. (1999). *Reflective journal.* Unpublised manuscript.

Brown, L. (1999). *Reflective journal.* Unpublished manuscript.

Boyd, T. A. (1961). *Prophet of progress: Selections from the speeches of Charles F. Kettering.* New York: E. P. Dutton.

Bryan, C., & Reilley-Kaminski, K. (2002, April). *Effective parent communication: What does it look like?* Paper presented at the fourth annual State College Area School District–Pennsylvania State University Teacher Inquiry Conference, State College, PA.

Calkins, L. M. (1986). *The art of teaching writing.* Portsmouth, NH: Heinemann.

Carr, W., & Kemmis, S. (1986). *Becoming critical: Knowing through action research.* Geelong, Victoria: Deakin University Press.

Clark, C. (1995). *Thoughtful teaching.* New York: Teachers College Press.

Cochran-Smith, M. (1991). Learning to teach against the grain. *Harvard Educational Review, 61*(3), 279-310.

Cochran-Smith, M., & Lytle, S. L. (1993). *Inside/outside: Teacher research and knowledge.* New York: Teachers College Press.

Cochran-Smith, M., & Lytle, S. L. (1999). The teacher research movement: A decade later. *Educational Researcher, 28*(7), 15-25.

Cochran-Smith, M., & Lytle, S. L. (2001). Beyond certainty: Taking an inquiry stance on practice. In A. Lieberman & L. Miller (Eds.), *Teachers caught in the action: Professional development that matters* (pp. 45-58). New York: Teachers College Press.

Creswell, J. W. (1998). *Qualitative inquiry and research design.* Thousand Oaks, CA: Sage.

Dana, N. F. (1994). Building partnerships to effect educational change: School culture and the finding of teacher voice. In M. J. O'Hair & S. J. Odell (Eds.), *Partnerships in education: Teacher education yearbook II* (pp. 11-26). New York: Harcourt Brace College.

Dana, N. F. (1995). Action research, school change, and the silencing of teacher voice. *Action in Teacher Education, 16*(4) 59-70.

Dana, N. F. (1999). *The professional development school story: Assessing the impact of year one (1998-99) of the State College Area School District-Pennsylvania State University Elementary Professional Development Schools.* Research report submitted to The State College Area School District Board of Directors.

Dana, N. F. (2001, April). *Inquiry in the PDS: The thread that ties the content areas together.* Paper presented at the annual meeting of the American Educational Research Association, Seattle, WA.

Dana, N. F., Gimbert, B., & Silva, D. Y. (1999). Teacher inquiry: Staff development for the 21st century. *Pennsylvania Educational Leadership, 18*(2), 6-12.

Dana, N. F., & Silva, D. Y. (2001). Student teachers as researchers: Developing an inquiry stance towards teaching. In J. D. Rainer & E. M. Guyton (Eds.), *Research on the effects of teacher education on teacher performance* (pp. 91-104). Dubuque, Iowa: Kendall/Hunt.

Dana, N. F., & Silva, D. Y. (2002). Building an inquiry oriented PDS: Inquiry as a part of mentor teacher work. In I. N. Guadarrama, J. Nath, & J. Ramsey (Eds.), Forging alliances in community and thought: *Research in professional development schools.* Greenwich, CT: Information Age.

Dana, N. F., Silva, D. Y., Gimbert, B., Nolan, J., Zembal-Saul, C., Tzur, R., Mule, L., & Sanders, L. (2001). Developing new understandings of PDS work: Better problems, better questions. *Action in Teacher Education, 22*(4), 15-27.

Dana, N. F., Silva, D. Y., & Snow-Gerono, J. (2002). Building a culture of inquiry in a professional development school. *Teacher Education and Practice, 15* (4), 71-89.

Darling-Hammond, L. (1994). Developing professional development schools: Early lessons, challenge, and promise. In L. Darling-Hammond (Ed.), *Professional development schools: Schools for developing a profession* (pp. 1-27). New York: Teachers College Press.

Dempsie, G. (1997). Using puppets in a primary classroom: A teacher-researcher's findings. *Teaching and Learning: The Journal of Natural Inquiry, 11*(3), 5-13.

Dempsie, G. (2000). Can I love you? A child's adventure with puppets and play. *The Journal of the Imagination in Language Learning, 5,* 28-36.

Derman-Sparks, L. (1989). *Anti-bias curriculum: Tools for empowering young children.* Washington, DC: National Association for the Education of Young Children.

Dewey, J. (1933). *Democracy and education.* New York: Free Company.

Dickinson, V., & Young, T. (1998). Elementary science and language arts: Should we blur the boundaries? *School Science and Mathematics, 98*(6), 334-339.

Elliot, J. (1988). Educational research and outsider–insider relations. *Qualitative Studies in Education, 1*(2), 155-166.

Ely, M. (1996). *Doing qualitative research: Circles within circles.* Philadelphia: Falmer.

Frank, M. (1979). *If you're trying to teach kides how to write, you've gotta have this book!* Nashville,TN: Incentive.

Frankes, L., Valli, L., & Cooper, D. H. (1998). Continuous learning for all adults in the professional development school: A review of research. In D. J. McIntyre and D. M. Byrd (Eds.) *Strategies for career-long teacher education: Teacher Education Yearbook VI* (pp. 69-83). Thousand Oaks, CA: Corwin.

Garman, Q. (1997, Fall). The slap heard 'round the room. *Partnership News (Newsletter of the Pennsylvania State University College of Education)*, 1-4.

Glanz, J. (1998). *Action research: An educational leader's guide to school improvement.* Norwood, MA: Christopher-Gordon.

Glaser, B. (1978). *Theoretical sensitivity: Advances in the methocology of grounded theory.* Mill Valley, CA: Sociology Press.

Goldhammer, R. (1969). *Clinical supervision: Special methods for the supervision of teachers.* New York: Holt, Rinehart & Winston.

Goodlad, J. I. (1990). *Teachers for our nation's schools.* San Francisco: Jossey-Bass.

Greene, M. (1986). Reflections and passion in teaching. *Journal of Curriculum and Supervision, 2*(1) 68-81.

Hall, J. (1998). *Organizing wonder: Making inquiry science work in the elementary school.* Portsmouth, NH: Heinemann.

Hampton, D., & Schickel, B. (2002, April). *Phonemic awareness: A key to kindergarten.* Paper presented at the fourth annual State College Area School District–Pennsylvania State University Teacher Inquiry Conference, State College, PA.

Holmes Group. (1986). *Tomorrow's teachers: A report of the Holmes Group.* East Lansing, MI: Author.

Holmes Group. (1990). *Tomorrow's schools: Principles for the design of professional development schools.* East Lansing, MI: Author.

Hosfeld, A. (2000, April). *Implementing anti-bias curriculum: Addressing the needs and constraints of an elementary classroom.* Paper presented at the second annual State College Area School District–Pennsylvania State University Teacher Inquiry Conference, State College, PA.

Hubbard, R. S., & Power, B. M. (1993). *The art of classroom inquiry: A handbook for teacher researchers.* Portsmouth, NH: Heinemann.

Hubbard, R. S., & Power, B. M. (1999). *Living the questions: A guide for teacher researchers.* York, ME: Stenhouse.

Jacobs, F. (1992). *The Tainos: The people who welcomed Columbus.* New York: G. P. Putman.

Jones, A., & Reed, D. (2000, April). *Rethinking Columbus.* Paper presented at the second annual State College Area School District–Pennsylvania State University Teacher Inquiry Conference, State College, PA.

Kincheloe, J. (1991). *Teachers as researchers: Qualitative inquiry as a path to empowerment.* New York: Falmer.

Koziak, M., & Abruzzo, S. (2000, April). *Effective parent–teacher communication: Enhancing the teaching partnership between home and school.* Paper presented at the second annual State College Area School District–Pennsylvania State University Teacher Inquiry Conference, State College, PA.

Kur, J. (2000, April). *Dinosaurs in the primary classroom: From facts and crafts to inquiry.* Paper presented at the second annual State College Area School

District–Pennsylvania State University Teacher Inquiry Conference, State College, PA.

Loewen, J. (1995). *Lies my teacher told me: Everything your American history text-book got wrong.* New York: New Press.

Lessem, D. (1991, May 19). The great dinosaur rip-off. *New York Times.*

Lortie, D. C. (1975). *School teacher: A sociological study.* Chicago: University of Chicago Press.

Lunsford, S. (1998). *Literature-based mini-lessons to teach writing.* New York: Scholastic Professional Books.

Malaggese, L. (2001, April). *What is a fair share? And other fractional adventures in a first grade classroom.* Paper presented at the third annual State College Area School District–Pennsylvania State University Teacher Inquiry Conference, State College, PA.

Marshall, C., & Rossman, G. B. (1999). *Designing qualitative research* (3rd ed.). Thousand Oaks, CA: Sage.

McCarty, C., & Poehner, P. (2002, April). *Peer coaching in an elementary classroom.* Paper presented at the fourth annual State College Area School District–Pennsylvania State University Teacher Inquiry Conference, State College, PA.

Mills, G. E. (2003). *Action research: A guide for the teacher resarcher.* Saddle River, NJ: Pearson Education, Inc.

Mitchell, K. (2000, April). *How do airplanes fly? (How do I become a more effective science teacher?).* Paper presented at the second annual State College Area School District–Pennsylvania State University Teacher Inquiry Conference, State College, PA.

Martchenko, M., & Munsch, R. N. (1988). *The paperbag princess.* New York: Annick Press.

Munsart, C. A. (1993). *Investigating science with dinousaurs.* Englewood, CO: Teacher Ideas Press.

Niebauer, H. (1997, Fall). Learning, not control. *Partnership News (Newsletter of the Pennsylvania State University College of Education,* pp. 10-11.

National Parent and Teachers Association (PTA). (1997). *National standards for parent/family involvement programs* (booklet) [On-line]. Available: http://www.pta.org.

Nolan, J. F., & Huber, T. (Winter, 1989). Nurturing the reflective practitioner through instructional supervision: A review of the literature. *Journal of Curriculum and Supervision, 4*(2), 126-145.

Patton, M. Q. (2002). *Qualitative research & evaluation methods* (3rd ed.). Thousand Oaks, CA: Sage.

Peters, B., & Romig, G. (2001, April). *Let's talk about science.* Paper presented at the third annual State College Area School District–Pennsylvania State University Teacher Inquiry Conference, State College, PA.

Pinkney, J., & Andersen, H.C. (1999). *The ugly duckling.* New York: Morrow Junior Press.

Quindlen, A. (1997). *Happily ever after.* New York: Random House.

Richert, A. E. (1997). Teaching teachers for the challenge of change. In J. Loughran & T. Russell (Eds.), *Teaching about teaching: Purpose, passion, and pedagogy in teacher education* (pp. 73-94). Washington, DC: The Falmer Press.

Roberts, R., & Elliot, L. (2002, April). *Taking a look at inquiry through inquiry.* Paper presented at the fourth annual State College Area School District–Pennsylvania State University Teacher Inquiry Conference, State College, PA.

Rotz, L., Kur, J., Robert, M., & Heitzmann, M. (2002, April). *Getting smarter with smartboards: A collaborative project.* Paper presented at the fourth annual State College Area School District–Pennsylvania State University Teacher Inquiry Conference, State College, PA.

Routman, R. (2002). *Conversations: Strategies for teaching, learning, and evaluating.* Portsmouth, NH: Heinemann.

Russell, J. L. (2002, April). *Once upon a writer's workshop: Using children's literature to inspire dazzling, complete stories.* Paper presented at the fourth annual State College Area School District–Pennsylvania State University Teacher Inquiry Conference, State College, PA.

Ruth, A. (1999, May). *The kindergarten writing center: Providing opportunities for an ESL student's language growth and development.* Paper presented at the first annual State College Area School District–Pennsylvania State University Teacher Inquiry Conference, State College, PA.

Ruth, A. (2001, April). *Two journeys of exploration.* Paper presented at the third annual State College Area School District–Pennsylvania State University Teacher Inquiry Conference, State College, PA.

Ruth, A. (2002, April). *Wanted: A new approach to using the minutes between 8:30 and 9:00 a.m. in my classroom.* Paper presented at the fourth annual State College Area School District–Pennsylvania State University Teacher Inquiry Conference, State College, PA.

Schon, D. (1987). *Educating the reflective practitioner.* San Francisco: Jossey-Bass.

Schon, D. A. (1983). *The reflective practitioner.* San Francisco: Jossey-Bass.

Schwandt, T. A. (1997). *Qualitative inquiry: A dictionary of terms.* Thousand Oaks, CA: Sage.

Sherman, R. R., & Webb, R. B. (1997). *Qualitative research in education: Focus and methods.* Philadelphia: Falmer.

Shulman, L. (1986). Knowledge and teaching: Foundations of the new reform. *Harvard Educational Review, 57*(1), 1-22.

Silva, D. Y., & Dana, N. F. (1999, February). *Cultivating inquiry within a professional development school.* Presentation at the annual meeting of the American Association of Colleges for Teacher Education, Washington, D.C.

Silva, D. Y., & Dana, N. F. (2001). Collaborative supervision in the professional development school. *Journal of Curriculum and Supervision, 16*(4), 305-321.

Silva, D. Y., & Dana, N. F. (2000, April). *Creating spaces for new roles, responsibilities, and relationships: An ethnographic case study of teachers' work in a professional development school.* Presentation at the annual meeting of the American Educational Research Association, New Orleans, LA.

Snow, J. L., Dana, N. F., & Silva, D. Y. (2001). Where are they now? Former PDS interns emerge as first year teacher leaders. *The Professional Educator, 24*(1), 35-48.

Sunner, N. (1999, May). *Questioning.* Paper presented at the first annual State College Area School District–Pennsylvania State University Teacher Inquiry Conference, State College, PA.

Stiles, P. (1999). *Reflective journal.* Unpublished manuscript.

Strauss, A., & Corbin, J. (1998). *Basics of qualitative research.* Thousand Oaks, CA: Sage.

Stringer, E. T. (1996). *Action research: A handbook for practitioners.* Thousand Oaks, CA: Sage.

Thulin, J. (1999, May). *Meaningful melodies: Reading to the beat of a different drummer.* Paper presented at the first annual State College Area School District-Pennsylvania State University Teacher Inquiry Conference, State College, PA.

Wilson, S. M., Floden, R. E., & Ferrini-Mundy, J. (2001). *Teacher preparation research: Current knowledge, gaps, recommendations.* A research report prepared for the U.S. Department of Education and the Office for Education Research and Improvement. University of Washington: Center for the Study of Teaching and Policy.

Wolcott, H. F. (1990). *Writing up qualitative research.* Newbury Park, CA: Sage.

Wolcott, H. F. (1994). *Transforming qualitative data: Description, analysis, and interpretation.* Thousand Oaks, CA: Sage.

Zeichner, K. (1986). Preparing reflective teachers: An overview of instructional strategies which have been employed in preservice teacher education. *International Journal of Educational Research, 7*(5), 565-575.

Zeichner, K. (1996). Teachers as reflective practitioners and the democratization of school reform. In K. Zeichner, S. Melnick, & M. L. Gomez (Eds.), *Currents of reform in preservice teacher education* (pp. 199-214). New York: Teacher College Press.

Zeichner, K. M., & Liston, D. P. (1996). *Reflective teaching: An introduction.* Mahway, NJ: Lawrence Erlbaum.

Index

**CORWIN
PRESS**

The Corwin Press logo—a raven striding across an open book—represents the happy union of courage and learning. We are a professional-level publisher of books and journals for K-12 educators, and we are committed to creating and providing resources that embody these qualities. Corwin's motto is "Success for All Learners."